Periscope

See Above. Live Beyond

A 49 Day Journey to Living a Transformed Life

Kerby Anderson

We hope you enjoy this book from Probe Ministries. For more information on this subject and related topics from a Christian worldview perspective, please visit us at www.probe.org. For more on this series, you can go to www.upPeriscope.org.

Library of Congress Cataloging-in-Publication Data

Anderson, Kerby

Periscope: A 49 Day Journey to Living a Transformed Life / Kerby Anderson – 1st ed.

p. cm.
Includes bibliographical references

ISBN 978-0-945241-22-5

Endorsements:

We live in a world of chaos and darkness because Christians have been ineffective. They have failed to advance God's kingdom. That's why I am excited about the new church program: *Periscope: See Above, Live Beyond*. The book, along with sermons, music, and videos empower Christians to become a positive influence for good in the midst of darkness and despair. I encourage your church or small group to begin this 49-day transformative journey. Your church and the community will be better for it.

Dr. Tony Evans
Senior Pastor, Oak Cliff Bible Fellowship
President, The Urban Alternative

Many Christians need help in living free from cultural captivity, and that is why I am excited about the new study experience, *Periscope: See Above, Live Beyond*. Probe Ministries taught this material in our Sunday night Discipleship University. Members of our congregation greatly appreciated the teaching, videos, and small group interaction. I recommend it to your church or small group.

Dr. Robert Jeffress
Senior Pastor,
First Baptist Church, Dallas, Texas

My friend, Kerby Anderson, continues to impact the culture for Christ and provide resources to equip Believers and churches in advancing the Word of God. His latest, *Periscope*, is an invaluable tool designed to address the millennial generation and the need to live from an eternal perspective. I highly recommend it.

Dr. Jack Graham
Pastor, Prestonwood Baptist Church

I can't think of anything more important for a Christian than perspective: who we are, why we are here, what is my purpose, who are my enemies, etc. Each section of Kerby's study is non-negotiable and absolute – no Christian can live properly in ignorance of these areas. To focus them all in a 49-day journey with a small group to support and encourage is an invaluable experience and tool for the rest of one's life. This material is simple, basic but absolutely vital. What's better, it is transferable and can be passed onto someone else.

Tommy Nelson
Senior Pastor, Denton Bible Church

The research by Probe Ministries has demonstrated that a very small percentage of the current generation has a biblical worldview that they consistently apply to biblical beliefs and practice. If this trend continues, we will have fewer churches, fewer Christian organizations, and fewer missionaries. At East-West Ministries, we train missionaries to be effective in foreign cultures. We need missionaries to our own culture and need to free Christians from cultural captivity. That is why I am excited about the *Periscope* church program and recommend it to your church or small group.

John Maisel
Founder and Chairman Emeritus,
East-West Ministries

Periscope is a Bible Study with difference. Current topics are addressed through the lens of Scripture to help a younger generation navigate their way through our present powerful cultural attitudes and assumptions. No one does this better than Kerby Anderson who has been addressing these issues for many years. Those who reflect on these studies will have practical insights on both the teaching of the Bible and the seductive but erroneous beliefs of our modern world.

Dr. Erwin W. Lutzer
Pastor Emeritus
The Moody Church, Chicago

Few Christians experience the transformation that could be theirs. Too many remain captive to false concepts that put a ceiling on their spiritual power. Kerby Anderson guides readers through a 49-day transformative journey from cultural captivity to spiritual confidence. With clear, concise, short chapters he unpacks biblical truth that opens our eyes to see what's above, and thus how to live a fuller life for Christ today. I wish every person in our church would read this book and put it into practice. Many are not even aware they are cultural captives, much less able to envision being confident ambassadors for Christ. Anderson frees us from captivity and sends us out as Christ's representatives.

Bruce B. Miller
Senior Pastor, Christ Fellowship
Author, *Your Life in Rhythm* and more

Probe Ministries, under the able leadership of Kerby Anderson, has produced one of the most helpful resources for churches and small groups that I've ever seen. Titled "*Periscope*," this program is relevant, accessible, and highly transformational in nature. Two thumbs way up!

Dr. Ron Rhodes, Christian Author

For more than 40 years Kerby Anderson and Probe Ministries has opened the minds of Americans to the eternal truths of God's Word in an unparalleled manner. Simply put, Probe Ministries under Kerby's leadership has set the standard for those wanting to experience the power of God that comes only from first knowing the Word and then obeying it. When I have a question and need clarity I pray, then I call my friend and colleague Kerby!

Gary Frazier, Discovery Missions

Kerby Anderson does it again! If grace and truth are twin attributes of God reflected in the godly, Kerby models both in his ministry and his writings. *Periscope* is another critical chapter in his life narrative of presenting the conviction of a biblical faith with a keen mind and a compassionate heart. This book helps us to rise above the chaos and catch a fresh look at God's perspective as to how to live in a self-conflicting world.

Mark L. Bailey, Ph.D.
President,
Dallas Theological Seminary

Table of Contents

Introduction

Welcome to Periscope. We want to help you see above and live beyond. Satan and the world want to deceive us into viewing this world as the sum total of our existence. As a Christian, nothing could be further from the real truth. This material is a 49-day challenge that will help you see the world from an eternal perspective and begin to live in ways that honor God and enable you to experience all that He has for you in the Christian life.

One of the biggest roadblocks to seeing the world correctly is cultural captivity. In Colossians 2:8 Paul warns Christians: "See to it that no one takes you captive through philosophy and empty deception, according to the tradition of men, according to the elementary principles of the world, rather than according to Christ." We should be on the alert not to be taken captive by the culture.

This comprehensive experience consists of sermons, music, videos, emails, voice mails, text messages and more with the intent of surrounding you with a common theme: God has called you to live as a citizen of heaven temporarily on this earth for His purpose. It is my prayer this experience will be instrumental in helping you live a fuller and more meaningful life for Christ.

This book consists of 49 chapters. You should read one chapter each day for these seven weeks. The emails, voice mails, and text messages serve to reinforce what you have read for that day. The first chapter should be read a week in advance of the small group meeting with the seventh chapter being read on the day of your small group meeting.

I am thrilled that you will be reading this book. My prayer is that what you will be learning in the next few weeks will free you from areas of cultural captivity that you might have in your life. I also pray that all of us will apply what we learn to our daily lives.

James 1:22 admonishes each of us to "prove yourselves doers of the word, and not merely hearers." This book and the entire Periscope experience are intended to change our lives so that we are freed from cultural captivity (Colossians 2:8) and empowered to be confident ambassadors for Christ (2 Corinthians 5:20).

Chapter 1: Growing Stronger

2nd Corinthians 4:16 *So we do not lose heart. Though our outer self is wasting away, our inner self is being renewed day by day.*[1]

There is more to life than life. When you look through the periscope of God's perspective, you can glimpse eternity. You will live forever. And that makes all the difference in the world. You were made for more than just living a few years on earth before you die and cease to exist.

If you are young, you may not be thinking much about getting older and are probably not thinking much about your death. But it is a certain reality. And it can make a difference in how you live now, when you realize that you are an eternal being that actually will live forever.

People in our world are looking for purpose and meaning in their lives. But they will not find it by looking inward at themselves. They need to have the proper perspective. What they need, what we all need, is an eternal perspective.

We live in time and space, but we are headed for an eternal world outside of our current space/time dimensions. Therefore, if we are to see the world and our purpose accurately, we need an eternal perspective.

The Apostle Paul had such a perspective. He wrote, "I die daily."[2] He meant not only that he was no longer living for himself, but was also referring to the possibility of his own death (martyrdom). He was faced with the imminent reality of his own death, yet he was confident and encouraged.

In his second letter to the church in Corinth he says, "We are pressed on every side by troubles, but we are not crushed. We are perplexed, but not driven to despair."[3] Even in the midst of his trials, troubles, and threats, he could say, "We do not lose heart."[4]

Paul was on the edge of death all the time. He knew that each day could be his last. But he did not lose heart because he had an eternal perspective.

We may not be facing the trials that Paul did, but each day we do face trials. Our death may not be imminent, but each day we are one day closer to our death. How do we live a life of confidence and experience all that God has for us?

In this chapter, and the following chapters, let's look at Paul's perspective, his eternal perspective on life. He begins by describing three contrasts that keep him from losing heart.

An eternal perspective is key to true spiritual growth

Paul says, "Therefore we do not lose heart. Though outwardly we are wasting away, yet inwardly we are being renewed day by day."[5] This is the contrast between the outer person and the inner person. He says that though the outer person is decaying, the inner person is renewed day by day. We may be getting older and our outer person is in decline, but we should be growing inwardly. Theologians call this the process of sanctification.

The believer has an inner, spiritual life. The goal of the Christian life is to become more Christ-like. Yet many times Christians accept salvation and never grow much beyond that point. They see salvation as a ticket to heaven. Once they know they have that ticket, they go on about their lives without much regard to their inner, spiritual life.

Paul's teaching provides important lessons for us. First, the Christian life is to be lived daily. He says "we are being renewed day by day." We are to be spiritually renewed as we walk with Christ (a principle we will discuss in future chapters). When we have an eternal perspective our spiritual growth should continue throughout our lives.

C.S. Lewis uses an example of how we are affected by what is around us. "If you want to get warm you must stand near the fire: if you want to be wet you must get into the water. If you want joy, power, peace, eternal life, you must get close to, or even into, the thing that has them."[6] He reminds us that we must be near what we desire. He concludes by observing: "Once a man is united to God, how could he not live forever? Once a man is separated from God, what can he do but wither and die?"[7]

A second principle is that we are all getting older. Growing older every day, being one day closer to our death can be depressing if we merely live for this world. An eternal perspective helps us have a proper understanding of our place in God's world. One writer humorously describes the seven decades of life this way: spills, drills, thrills, bills, ills, pills, wills. Whatever stage of life we are in, we need an eternal perspective.

John Quincy Adams was the son of a president and then also served as president of the United States. On his eightieth birthday, a friend asked him "How is John Quincy Adams?" The former president replied, "John Quincy Adams is well, sir, quite well, I thank you. But the house in which he lives at present is becoming dilapidated. It is tottering upon the foundations. Time and the seasons have nearly destroyed it. Its roof is pretty well worn out, its walls are shattered, and it trembles with every wind. The old tenement is becoming almost uninhabitable, and I think John Quincy Adams will have to move out of it soon; but he himself is quite well, sir, quite well."

We may be growing older physically, but we should also be growing stronger spiritually. Paul describes a contrast between the outer person and the inner person. In our next chapter, we explain a second contrast that gives us an eternal perspective.

Grow stronger spiritually while decaying physically

Chapter 2: The Weight of Glory

2nd Corinthians 4:17 *For our light and momentary troubles are achieving for us an eternal glory that far outweighs them all."*[8]

The Apostle Paul wrote that he did not lose heart even in the midst of the trials, troubles, and threats. He explains three contrasts that helped him to maintain an eternal perspective. The previous chapter explained his contrast between the inner person and the outer person. The second was a contrast between his troubles and eternal glory.

In our verse for today, it is amazing that Paul referred to what he was facing as light and momentary troubles. Some translations use the word affliction: "For momentary, light affliction is producing for us an eternal weight of glory far beyond all comparison." But even there, it still has the descriptions of affliction as light and momentary.

How can Paul call what he went through or what we are going through today, light and momentary? He was not minimizing troubles or afflictions. After all, he had been beaten, shipwrecked, and imprisoned.

What he is saying is that what from our earthly perspective seems heavy, hurtful, and grievous, will seem light and momentary when laid down next to glory. This is why we need an eternal perspective. What seems so overwhelming right now lessens in its pain and impact when compared to an eternal weight of glory.

As we live our lives here on earth, we should increase our eternal weight of glory. As we grow as Christians, we honor the Lord and lay up treasures in heaven.[9] In fact, it could be said that the tougher it is down here, the more our eternal glory should weigh up there.

In his letter to the Christians in Rome, Paul makes a similar statement. He says, "For I consider that the sufferings of this present time are not worthy to be compared with the glory that is to be revealed to us."[10]

Notice the order. First, there is suffering, then there is glory. This was true for Jesus Christ, and it will be true for us as well. He was the suffering servant in His first coming. He will be the King of Kings, and Lord of Lords in his second coming.

Also, notice that this future glory will be "revealed to us." Glory is in our future, while trials and troubles are in our present. An eternal perspective can keep these two contrasts in mind, especially since that glory is not presently seen but will unfold before our eyes in the future.

> *Glory is in our future, while trials and troubles are in our present.*

The Apostle Peter talked about how our faith is refined by trials and suffering. He explains that our faith is "of greater worth than gold, which perishes even though refined by fire—may be proved genuine and may result in praise, glory and honor when Jesus Christ is revealed."[11]

Before we conclude, let me quote from C.S. Lewis who wrote about "The Weight of Glory." It was originally preached as a sermon in 1942 and it reminds us of the need to have an eternal perspective in every area of life. It will help us see the world as God sees it, and it will help us deal with other people in a way that honors God.

"It is a serious thing to live in a society of possible gods and goddesses, to remember that the dullest and most uninteresting person you talk to may one day be a creature which, if you saw it now, you would be strongly tempted to worship, or else a horror and a corruption such as you now meet, if at all, only in a nightmare. All day long we are, in some degree, helping each other to one or other of these destinations. It is in the light of these overwhelming possibilities, it is with the awe and the circumspection proper to them, that we should conduct all our dealings with one another, all friendships, all loves, all play, all politics. There are no ordinary people. You have never talked to a mere mortal. Nations, cultures, arts, civilization – these are mortal, and their life is to ours as the life of a gnat. But it is immortals whom we joke with, work with, marry, snub, and exploit – immortal horrors or everlasting splendors." [12]

An eternal perspective reminds us that not only will we live forever, but everyone we meet will live forever. If we were to see them now in their future state, C.S. Lewis tells us we would be tempted to worship them or turn away from them depending on their destiny.

An eternal perspective reminds us that there are no mere mortals. The world we see around us is temporal. The real world is the unseen world. That is a perspective we discuss in the next chapter.

The real world is unseen and eternal.

Chapter 3: The Unseen World

2nd Corinthians 4:18 *So we fix our eyes not on what is seen, but on what is unseen. For what is seen is temporary, but what is unseen is eternal.*[13]

The three contrasts that Paul describes helped him not to lose heart. The first contrast was between the outer person and the inner person. The second was between troubles or affliction and an eternal weight of glory. His third contrast is between the seen world and the unseen world.

Our verse for today introduces the contrast between the temporal and the eternal, or the seen world and the unseen world.

Many times in the Bible we are admonished to place our faith in the unseen. The writer of the book of Hebrews says that faith is the conviction of things not seen.[14] By faith, we have a certainty of things that are invisible. We know that there is a world that is real, perhaps we could say, even more real than the world we see around us.

Skeptics often ridicule the idea of believing in something you cannot see. But try to find an astronomer who doesn't believe in the existence of black holes. No one can see a black hole, yet scientist believe they exist because of the evidence. Likewise, we may not be able to see an unseen world, but we have evidence through revelation (the Bible, the person of Jesus Christ, etc.) for the existence of a reality we presently cannot see.

The Bible teaches that there is much more to the world than what we can see. This shouldn't be a problem for modern science. The microscope has allowed us to see in the small dimensions of space. The telescope provides a more accurate view of the large dimensions of space. The Bible offers a perspective we cannot see. There is a world beyond our world.

The great Bible teacher A.W. Tozer used to say that the invisible world described in the Bible was the only real world.

An important question we should be asking is, "What is God doing that I cannot see?" An eternal perspective helps us see what God is doing in the world and helps us seek His will in our lives.

An eternal perspective helps order our priorities.

An eternal perspective that understands there is an unseen world helps us order our priorities. The biographies of many wealthy men and women tell the story of people who have gained the whole world, yet lost their souls. They have been laying up treasures on earth rather than laying up treasures in heaven.[15] The Jewish Talmud puts it this way: "Man is born with his hands clenched; he dies with his hands wide open. Entering life he desires to grasp everything; leaving the world, all that he possessed has slipped away."

Perhaps you have heard the statement that many of us spend our entire lives climbing the ladder of success only to find that it was leaning on the wrong wall. An eternal perspective provides guidance so that we don't spend our lives pursuing that which will not satisfy and simply fade away.

One of the songs in the *Now I'm Bound* CD that accompanies this teaching program is "One True God."[16] The lyrics remind us that the seen world will pass away in the future. We need to focus on what is important, in light of eternity.

When the dust has settled and this world is no more
Every saint and sinner will confess that you are Lord
Some will kneel as children, some as conquered foes
Everyone from every age will bow before the throne of the
One True God
The King who reigns on high

No one will deny – you are the
One True God
Earthly kings and kingdoms rise and have their day
Like a mist they linger then forever fade away
There is none so mighty, not one that compares to your
Majesty and glory
Lord, the universe declares you are
Awesome and holy, faithful and able, matchless and mighty

The three contrasts we have discussed in these chapters were part of what Paul understood to be essential elements of an eternal perspective that keeps us from losing heart. He also describes four eternal characteristics that provide spiritual direction and spiritual encouragement. Let's now look at each of these in the next four chapters.

Don't spend your life pursuing that which will not last or satisfy.

Chapter4: Eternal Body

2nd Corinthians 5:1-4 *Now we know that if the earthly tent we live in is destroyed, we have a building from God, an eternal house in heaven, not built by human hands. Meanwhile we groan, longing to be clothed with our heavenly dwelling, because when we are clothed, we will not be found naked. For while we are in this tent, we groan and are burdened, because we do not wish to be unclothed but to be clothed with our heavenly dwelling, so that what is mortal may be swallowed up by life.*

In addition to the three contrasts that Paul describes, he also explains a number of attributes of our eternal circumstances. He says, in the verse above for example, that we will have an eternal body. He begins by saying that "we groan." This is a reference back to the process of aging. We carry burdens through our lives that seem to increase as we get older. We have physical burdens, burdens of age, burdens of illness, burdens of disappointment and failure. When Paul wrote to Christians in Rome, he said: "For we know that the whole creation groans and suffers the pains of childbirth together until now."[17]

He also calls our body an "earthly tent." It is easy to see why Paul would use that imagery. He was a tent-maker by trade[18] and probably thought about how our bodies were like a tent. A tent is temporary and sometimes fragile or frail, especially in a storm. Tents also were significant to the Israelites. They had lived around nomads who moved from place to place. They would put up a tent, and then they would move on. They did not have a permanent home.

They might have also thought of a larger tent: the tabernacle. Here is where God's presence was. But again it moved from place to place until the Holy of Holies was placed in the Temple.

The implications for us are significant. We may feel like the world is our home, but we are destined for a future home. So we are much like the nomads who move from place to place but never really own the land. We are sojourners in the land until we go to our final home. But as we live on earth, we have God in the form of the Holy Spirit living within us.

Paul's description of our bodies as an earthly tent shows how he longed for a heavenly dwelling or an eternal body. How different is his attitude from ours today. Most of us have become comfortable with our earthly tent and even forget that it is merely a tent. What we experience today will pass away, but we often forget how transitory life can be.

We often forget how transitory life really is.

A tent has no foundations. It is temporary, not permanent. It can be blown away in the wind storm. What seems stable to us today could be gone tomorrow. Eternity is a lot longer than the 70+ years that most of us will spend on earth. As we talked about in the previous chapter, what we see is temporary. The unseen world is eternal. An eternal perspective helps us keep the eternal world in our minds. It helps order our priorities.

At our death, it is a time to take down the tent. The last words of Robert E. Lee were reported to be "strike the tent." This is a military term that was used meaning to take down the tent and move on. Lee was a man of faith so it is possible that he viewed his own death as a time to take down the tent and move on to the next life. At our death, we move out of our earthly tent (this earthly body we currently inhabit) and move into God's presence. Then we shall have an eternal body.

Notice that Paul uses the conditional word "if" as he talks about our earthy tent being destroyed. He says, "We know that if." Obviously the "we" applies to believers. But why does Paul say if? He is looking forward to the return of Christ, and therefore hopes that he (or his readers) might not face death. This is the blessed hope of Christ's return that we are to look to even today.

Chapter 5: Eternal Purpose

2nd Corinthians 5:5 . *Now it is God who has made us for this very purpose and has given us the Spirit as a deposit, guaranteeing what is to come.*[19]

Not only does Paul teach that we will have an eternal body, but we will also have an eternal purpose. What is your purpose in life? That may be a difficult question to answer. Ask a few people that question, and you will get interesting answers. Some may have an answer that has been thought through and seriously considered. Most will not have a good answer. Many will have no answer at all.

There should be a purpose to our lives. Fading mortality is not without design. A Christian should be doing more than just marking time in this life. There should be a purpose to what we do. An eternal perspective will give us that purpose.

Often we merely fill our lives with activities. And if this life is all that there is, then we probably should cram our lives with things and experiences. Consider these lines from two different films that demonstrate a vastly different perspective.

The 1989 film, "Dead Poets Society," is set at an all-boys preparatory school in Vermont. Their new English teacher uses unorthodox methods to encourage them in their studies and in life. He leads the students into the hallway to show them class photos of students in the past who have now died. They are "food for worms" and "fertilizing daffodils." He then uses the Latin phrase "carpe diem" which means to "seize the day." In essence, he is saying that this life is all there is. You live; you die; you are dirt. Therefore, you must seize the day, because this life is all that there is.

Contrast this perspective with the film, "Gladiator." In the opening scene General Maximus Decimus Meridius is about to lead soldiers of the Roman army into a battle against German barbarians. Their victory ends the long war on the Roman frontier. Before he leads them into battle he says: "What you do today, echoes through eternity." Even though he says this as a Roman soldier, the idea is certainly a Christian concept. What we do today in work, in our family, in our community echoes through eternity.

When you have an eternal perspective and an eternal purpose, you will also have biblical priorities. We see that in the life of Moses, who was willing to choose "to endure ill-treatment with the people of God than to enjoy the passing pleasures of sin."[20]

God prepared us for a purpose. Important questions to ask yourself are: What is God's purpose in your life? What purpose does God have for your actions and relationships?

One purpose is for us to proclaim Him to the world. The Apostle Peter says we are "a chosen race, a royal priesthood, a holy nation, a people for God's own possession, so that you may proclaim the excellencies of Him who has called you out of darkness into His marvelous light."[21]

God' purpose for you took place in eternity past. All that happens is according to His purpose. Paul says that "God causes all things to work together for good to those who love God, to those who are called according to His purpose."[22]

God planned our purpose in eternity past. He calls for us to follow His purpose in our lives on this earth. And we will see the fulfillment of His purpose in eternity future. We live in time following His purpose in our lives with eternity as bookends on what we do for Him today.

Our key purpose is to bring eternity to others.

Chapter 6: Eternal Fellowship

2nd Corinthians 5:6 *Therefore we are always confident and know that as long as we are at home in the body we are away from the Lord.*[23]

As we have seen in previous chapters, Paul teaches us that we will have an eternal body and an eternal purpose. We will also have eternal fellowship.

Paul writes that he does not lose heart. He can also be confident and encouraged because he knows that to be absent from the body is to be present with the Lord. Elsewhere he writes that "to live is Christ, to die is gain."[24]

Why does he say that? Paul knew that although we have temporary fellowship with believers here on earth, we are destined to have eternal fellowship with the Lord and with all believers. While we may enjoy the fellowship we have now, it will pale in comparison with our eternal fellowship.

We should live with an eternal perspective that looks forward to the eternal fellowship we will have. Peter instructs us to "fix your hope completely on the grace to be brought to you at the revelation of Jesus Christ."[25] We should live our lives focused on the future.

Paul put it this way. "Set your mind on things above and not on things that are on earth."[26] Again, we see he is challenging us to have an eternal perspective. He also says that we should reduce all that we think or do to one thing: "forgetting what lies behind and reaching forward to what lies ahead, I press on toward the goal for the prize of the upward call of God in Christ Jesus."[27] We should live with a perspective of what it will be like to be face-to-face with Jesus.

Lots of questions surface whenever a conversation turns to heaven. Will I see my friends? Will I know my spouse? What will the fellowship of believers be like? Most of the questions are focused on our reunion with those who have died.

The most important questions should be: What will it be like to be in the presence of Jesus? Will we be eager to meet him? Or will we be ashamed of how we lived our lives? Our eternal fellowship with Him in the future should affect the way we live our lives today.

Notice that Paul says he was confident. Why was he confident? Because he knew that to be absent from the body is to be in the presence of the Lord. He looked forward to his new eternal body and longed for the perfection of eternity. But he also knew that God had a plan for him on earth. He had courage in the face of death and faced it with confidence. If he remained on earth, it was for Him to serve the Lord. If he died, he would experience eternal fellowship.

Likewise, we should be confident. God has a plan for us on earth. And He has prepared a place for us in eternity when we will have eternal fellowship with Him.

We have a place prepared for us in eternity with our Savior

Finally, we should also note that the transition from earth to eternity is instantaneous. To be absent from the body is to *immediately* be in the presence of the Lord. The body may sleep but the soul does not. At the moment of our death, we are in the conscious presence of the Lord. Our eternal fellowship begins immediately.

Chapter 7: Eternal Fulfillment

2nd Corinthians 5:7-10 *We live by faith, not by sight. We are confident, I say, and would prefer to be away from the body and at home with the Lord. So we make it our goal to please him, whether we are at home in the body or away from it. For we must all appear before the judgment seat of Christ, that each one may receive what is due him for the things done while in the body, whether good or bad.*[28]

The culmination of each of these eternal characteristics is eternal fulfillment. Paul would prefer to be with the Lord, but he also understands that God may have more for him to do on earth. He is ready to go to heaven, but he perseveres in order to please the Lord.

How different this is from our perspective. Most of us aren't that eager to leave this world. A pastor one time decided to get his congregation involved in his sermon. So he shouted out, "Who is ready to go to heaven?" People raised their hands and shouted out. But he noticed a young boy in the front row crossing his arms and shaking his head. Thinking this might be a great sermon illustration, he asked the boy, "Don't you want to go to heaven some day?" The boy's face brightened and he said, "Oh yes, I want to go some day. I just thought you were taking up volunteers to go today."

Aren't we like that little boy? Yes, we want to go to heaven some day, but not today. Yet Paul was ready to go whenever the Lord called him to Himself.

Until he is called to heaven, what is Paul's purpose? His purpose is to please the Lord. Put simply, Paul's incredible perseverance in the Christian life was to please the Lord. Likewise, our ultimate goal in life should be to be pleasing to God.

Believers in previous centuries understood that. The Westminster Shorter Catechism begins with this question: What is the chief end of man? The answer is: Man's chief end is to glorify God, and to enjoy Him forever. We will have ultimate fulfillment in heaven. Our eternal destination will be a place where there is no more guilt, no more anxiety, and no more fear.

Heaven is not only a destination. It is a motivation. We will appear before the judgment seat of Christ and receive what is due to us. What we have done on earth will have eternal value. We aren't talking about salvation. A believer is already saved.

The judgment seat of Christ is not punitive. It does not exist to judge believers for sin. Instead, it is to provide rewards to believers for what they have done to build Christ's kingdom.

We would all agree that many things we do in life are worthless from the perspective of eternity. We aren't talking about sin, but things and activities that have no eternal value. But there are other things we do that do indeed have eternal value. Those will be rewarded in heaven. And that will provide eternal fulfillment.

What we do on earth will have an impact in eternity. That is why an eternal perspective is so important. It helps us make right choices and orders our priorities.

> *What we do on earth*
> *will have an impact in eternity.*

Chapter 8: Our Adversary

John 8:45 *Whenever (Satan) speaks a lie, he speaks from his own nature, for he is a liar and the father of lies.*

Although we may think we see the world clearly, the Bible warns us that we can be deceived. Our desire to live with ease and success in this life may seem more important than God's eternal purpose in our lives. We may be captive to Satan's deception.

One of the most important aspects of Satan's deception is to make people believe that he does not really exist. It is ironic that we live in a society where a majority believes in the existence of spiritual beings, but they don't believe in Satan as a real person. They may attribute evil in the world to human behavior or even evil forces, but they don't believe there is a fallen angel named Satan.

Many Christians think that belief in Satan is optional. They say that belief in Jesus is enough. But if you believe that Jesus was God then you have to believe that Satan exists. Satan is mentioned in the Gospels twenty-nine times. And in twenty-five of those references, Jesus is the one talking about Satan. It is also worth mentioning that every New Testament writer talks about Satan. Belief in Satan is not optional.

What does Jesus say about Satan? When confronting his accusers, Jesus says: "You are of your father the devil, and you want to do the desires of your father. He was a murderer from the beginning, and does not stand in the truth because there is no truth in him. Whenever he speaks a lie, he speaks from his own nature, for he is a liar and the father of lies. But because I speak the truth, you do not believe Me."[1]

Satan is a deceiver, so we should be careful not to be deceived by him and the philosophies of his world system. He is in control of the world. We can see the extent of his influence by the three titles used to describe him in the New Testament.

1. Ruler of the world – Jesus refers to Satan as "the ruler of the world" in three passages.[2] This means that he can use the elements of society and culture to achieve his evil ends in this world. We should therefore be careful not to be conformed to the culture or become captive to the culture.[3]

2. God of this world – Paul refers to Satan as "the god of this world." He goes on to say that he "has blinded the minds of the unbelieving so that they might not see the light of the gospel of the glory of Christ, who is the image of God."[4] Spiritual blindness is another form of Satan's deception. It also means that Satan has set himself up as a false god to many in this world. He has the power to create and promote false religions keeping people from knowing the true gospel.

Satan has the power to create and promote false religions

3. Prince of the air – Paul reminds Christians that they were originally dead in their trespasses. At that time, they "walked according to the course of this world, according to the prince of the power of the air."[5] As the prince of the air, Satan can influence the thoughts of those in the world system. The Bible says: "The whole world lies in the power of the evil one."[6] He is more powerful than many of us give him credit, and so we should not be surprised when we see people who have been captured by deception.

We also learn a great deal about Satan from the names that are given to him. The name "Satan" in Hebrew means "adversary." He is opposed to God and His plans. And Satan is also opposed to God's plan in our lives. This characteristic of Satan is significant. The Old Testament uses this name for him eighteen times, and it is used thirty-four times in the New Testament.

Another name for Satan is "the devil." This name in the Greek is *diabolos* and is derived from the verb meaning "to throw." The Devil throws accusations and lies at us. This is a significant part of spiritual warfare. He accuses believers while he slanders and defames the name of God. This name occurs thirty-six times in the New Testament.

There is one passage in the New Testament that uses both of these names for Satan. Peter warns believers about Satan who is an "adversary" and "the devil" who is on the prowl like roaring lion.[7] This passage is a reminder that he is a formidable adversary.

Satan is also known as the "tempter." He tempts us to follow him and his evil ways rather than follow God's plan for our lives. When he appears to Jesus in the wilderness, he is referred to as the tempter (Matthew 4:3). Also, Paul refers to Satan as "the tempter" (1 Thessalonians 3:5) and thus illustrates one of the key characteristics of Satan. He tempts humans to sin.

We have a choice. Either we can believe God's truth or we can believe Satan's lies. We can accept God's grace or we can embrace Satan's counterfeits. In our next chapter we talk about what it means to follow God and walk in Christ.

> *Accept God's grace or embrace Satan's counterfeits.*
> *The choice is yours.*

Chapter 9: Walk in Christ

Colossians 2:6 *Therefore, as you have received Christ Jesus the Lord, so walk in Him*

In light of the threat of our being deceived in this world, it is so important for us to know how to prevent deception, resist temptation, and live the Christian life. Paul in his letters instructs us on how to avoid the snares of this world and live in accordance with God's plan for our lives.

In the book of Colossians, he begins by telling us of the hope we have in Christ and how we will inherit and experience eternal glory. Then in the second chapter he focuses on our present reality. He says: "Therefore, as you have received Christ Jesus the Lord, so walk in Him, having been firmly rooted and now being built up in Him and established in your faith, just as you were instructed, and overflowing with gratitude."[8]

Paul tells us that we are to walk in Christ. But before we can do that, we must be sure that we have received Christ. If we have not been reconciled to Christ and forgiven of our sins, then our Christian walk will be in neutral, even non-existent.

The Bible tells us that before we were saved, we were dead in our sins. "For all have sinned and come short of the glory of God."[9] The Bible also teaches that "even when we were dead in our transgressions" we were made alive through Christ. We are saved by grace "through faith and not of ourselves it is the gift of God and not of works lest any man should boast."[10] If you have not made this decision, then you must confess your sins and accept Christ's death on the cross and resurrection. You cannot walk in Christ until you have received Christ and put your trust in Him.

Paul's admonition is that we are to walk in Christ. In other places in the New Testament, we are called to "walk in the Spirit" and "walk in truth" and "walk in love." So how do we go about walking in Christ? Paul tells us that we have been rooted in Christ. That means we are being built up in Christ. This should be a real encouragement to us.

The world can be a difficult and disappointing place. First, we are tempted by the world, the flesh, and the devil.[11] Sometimes we can be overcome by the desires of the flesh.[12] As we discussed in the previous chapter, Satan can tempt us, accuse us, and deceive us. We are called to live a godly life in the midst of evil and error. We are to live a righteous life in the midst of unrighteousness.

That is why Paul's words can be encouraging to us. No matter how difficult it may be to live in this world, we have the clear teaching that we are "rooted in Christ." Here he is using an agricultural metaphor. God has placed our lives in the person of Jesus Christ. Your life and my life are rooted in Him. Your hope is grounded in His love, grace, and goodness. This can give us strength in times when we feel weak against the assault of the world, the flesh, and the devil.

Hope is grounded in His love, grace, and goodness

Not only are we rooted in Him, but we are even now being built up in Him. Paul now switches to a construction metaphor. In fact, the Greek word used here is a term that was often used to describe construction, the building up of something. Paul is telling us that we are being built up in our lives. The foundation is laid upon the gospel of Jesus Christ.[13] And he is now continuing that good work in us until the day He brings us into His presence.[14]

We may not feel like that is happening, but Paul assures us that it is taking place even if we feel we are taking backward steps in our walk in Christ. We are under construction, and God is working to bring us into conformity with Christ. One day we will be like Him for we shall see him as He is.[15]

It helps us to know that all that we are (body, soul, and spirit) is rooted in Christ. It is encouraging to know that we are being built up in Him. God is still working in us, conforming and shaping us so that we will look more like Jesus Christ.

Moreover, Paul says that we are also "being established" in our faith. The Greek word used here describes a legal contract. Essentially Paul is saying that Christ is legally bound to you and me. He has a legal document of ownership. You are His, and He is yours. This is one more guarantee of the steadiness of our walk in Christ. Is walking in Christ enough? Many verses (including the one we are currently discussing) remind us of the sufficiency of Christ.[16] Martin Luther once said: "Christ plus nothing equals everything."

C.S. Lewis put it this way: "He Himself is the fuel our spirits were designed to burn, or the food our spirits were designed to feed on. There is no other. That is why it is just no good asking God to make us happy in our own way without bothering about religion. God cannot give us a happiness and peace apart from Himself, because it is not there. There is no such thing."[17]

Finally, Paul provides a response to all that Christ has done for us. He says that he is "overflowing with gratitude." Thankfulness is the natural and obvious response to what Christ has done for us and is doing for us right this minute.

We are to walk in Christ and seek to be like Him as we turn away from our sin. One of the songs in the CD that accompanies this teaching program is "Let Our Worship Rise."[17] The lyrics challenge us to do just that.

We repent and turn away
From all our shame, from all our sin
To Your holiness, to Your holiness
Purify our hearts; burn away the sin
Start a fire in us; stir the flames again

9/19

Chapter 10: Captured by the Enemy

Colossians 2:8 *See to it that no one takes you captive through philosophy and empty deception, according to the tradition of men, according to the elementary principles of the world, rather than according to Christ*

Every war has stories of soldiers who were captured by the enemy because they weren't paying attention. They may have ignored warnings from more experienced men in the unit. They may have been easily deceived by the enemy's plan. Whatever the reason, the enemy was able to spring the trap and capture the soldiers. They were led away to captivity.

In the verse from Colossians at the top of the page, Paul issued a similar warning to Christians in the first century, and that warning is important for us to heed today. The religious environment then was similar to ours today. Various groups and forces were growing in popularity. Paul warned Christians not to be taken captive by those ideas. He was not talking about physical bars or chains. He was warning about invisible chains constraining our minds and causing us to think about the world contrary to biblical principles.

Whenever we assume that the perspective of the world is superior to the truth of Christ, we are allowing ourselves to be taken captive. We need to filter all truth claims through biblical revelation. Let's examine how Paul instructs us to keep from being held by the invisible chains of cultural captivity.

First, we must avoid capture by being on guard. We are to "see to it" we are not taken captive. In other words, we are to "beware" and "be careful." Like the unsuspecting soldier who falls into the trap of the enemy, we can fall into the traps laid by Satan and by those who oppose the Bible. It appears from what Paul wrote that the Christians had not yet fallen victim to false teachers, but their existence presented a clear and present danger.

Second, we must understand the consequences of capture. When we are captured by the enemy, we are taken away. We are the plunder or the booty that is removed. Likewise, captives of our culture are taken away to a place not of their choosing. Paul is not talking about Christians losing their salvation, but he is talking about the powerful forces that will take us away from the pure gospel.[18] As we will discuss in later chapters, Paul was warning them to avoid the legalism or asceticism that false teachers wanted to add to the gospel.

The warning against being taken captive is in the present tense. The danger of cultural captivity is an ever present threat. It is tempting to think that after you accept Jesus Christ, you have achieved total spiritual victory. As we discussed in the previous chapter, spiritual warfare is part of the Christian life. We must always be on the alert.[19] Satan does not just fight one battle. He fights a military campaign and will change methods of attack to achieve his ends.

The danger of cultural captivity is an ever present threat.

Paul also tells us what we must guard against in order to avoid being taken captive. He says we must guard against dangerous philosophies. That does not mean that Christians should never study philosophy. The word philosophy is a compound word that means "love of wisdom." Believers should love godly wisdom,[20] but they should reject the philosophies of the world. Many a Christian student has had his or her faith rocked by taking a philosophy class in a secular university taught by a professor who spent much of his class time attacking the Christian faith.

He not only identifies the danger of secular philosophy but also warns against "empty deception." The word empty implies an absence of anything substantive. Paul gives a similar warning to the Ephesians: "Let no one deceive you with empty words."[21] But these words and philosophies are not only empty, they are deceptive. They give a false impression. They may sound true and wise, but they are empty and deceive believers so they fall into cultural captivity.

Paul also warns them about the "traditions of men." He is not warning them to avoid all traditions. In other letters to Christians, he encourages them to "hold to the traditions you were taught."[22] On the other hand, Jesus rebuked the Pharisees because they were willing to "transgress the commandment of God for the sake of [their] tradition."[23] The false teachers were deceiving Christians into believing they must follow such practices as legalism, mysticism, and asceticism. Today false teachers and false ideas can capture us if we are not alert.

Finally, Paul warns that another source of false philosophy can come from "the elementary principles of the world." We could also refer to these as the first principles or the basic principles we find in our world. Later on in this passage he teaches that when we "have died with Christ" we have also died "to the elementary principles of the world."[24] We are living a spiritual life not just a physical life. He also explains in his letter to the Galatians that "we were children [and] were held in bondage under the elemental things of the world."[25] He is talking about the basic rituals of religious practice which are part of pagan worship and even Old Testament practices. Today false teachers promote cultic practices, eastern religion, and New Age philosophies.

Instead of being captured by the culture, we should be captured by Christ. We cannot allow ourselves to be captured by anything in the world. We must walk with Christ. He is "the way, the truth, and the life."[26] We are to depend on Him in order to avoid being led astray by false ideas and empty deception.

Be captured by Christ, not the culture.

Chapter 11: Weapons of the Enemy

Galatians 4:3 *In the same way we also, when we were children, were enslaved to the elementary principles of the world.*[27]

Because we are in a spiritual battle and because Satan is a powerful foe, we must be prepared for battle. And we must constantly make choices. Do we accept God's truth or do we accept Satan's lie? Usually the choice is not presented to us in such stark terms. Our enemy is subtle and deceptive. If we are to be victorious in the Christian life, we need to understand how he manipulates us. We need to understand his weapons in the spiritual war.

In the previous chapter we began with the warning Paul gave to Christians in the first century: "See to it that no one takes you captive through philosophy and empty deception, according to the tradition of men, according to the elementary principles of the world, rather than according to Christ."[28] He is reminding us that we can be influenced and deceived by the philosophies of this world. In his letter to the Galatians, Paul tells us that apart from Christ, we are held in bondage by the elementary principles of the world.[29]

In future chapters we will go into more detail about these false philosophies and principles that can capture us and keep us from living a dynamic Christian life. For a moment, let's look at some of these philosophies that Satan uses to distract us from the pure gospel. One is the philosophy of naturalism, which is the belief that we can explain everything in the world from a natural perspective. Neo-Darwinism is based upon the idea that strictly natural processes of random mutation and natural selection are responsible for the organisms in our world.

Another philosophy is legalism. Paul warns those attempting to take Christians captive through the subtle lies of legalism.[30] These false teachers were instructing Christians to go back and follow the laws of Moses. In our day there are teachers who want to bind Christians to the law or set forth a series of rules and regulations based upon the leader's prejudices not based upon biblical principles.

Paul also addresses mysticism by describing someone who drifts away by delighting in self-derived source of truths. These were "visions he has seen."[31] In our day, we have seen the explosion of interest among Christians in Eastern religions and the New Age Movement.

Captivity includes delighting in our own self-derived truths

And Paul also addresses asceticism, which is the doctrine of extreme self-denial. He warns Christians about false teachers who issue decrees such as: "Do not handle, do not taste, do not touch!"[32] Even in our day with an emphasis on pleasure, personal peace, and affluence, we have those who would teach that we are to remove our body from any pleasures in the world.

These are just a few of the false philosophies that the enemy uses to distract us from the truth of the Bible. We could add many other examples, but these few examples from Paul's letter to the Colossians provide an overview of the sort of weapons Satan uses against us.

Paul also talks about other types of attacks on our minds as strongholds. In one of his letters, Paul said: "We are destroying speculations and every lofty thing raised up against the knowledge of God, and we are taking every thought captive to the obedience of Christ."[33] If we think of our minds as a battlefield, then a stronghold would be a place on that battlefield that is reinforced and fortified.

What are some possible strongholds in our lives? Fear is one. Satan can hold us in bondage through fear and anxiety. Another might be depression and even thoughts of hopelessness and suicide.

Doubt is certainly a stronghold. We all know Christians who cannot live a vibrant and dynamic Christian life because they have doubts about their salvation, doubts about God, or doubts about the reliability of the Bible. We need to come alongside them and encourage them with biblical truth and the evidence for the Christian faith.

Some of the strongholds may be spiritual. Past involvement in the occult, demonic contact, or witchcraft can be used by Satan to hold someone in spiritual bondage.

Thoughts can become strongholds of Satan. He is a master at counterfeiting the truth of God's Word. In the next chapters, we will look at how he deceives us and how we are to fight a spiritual battle against him and be victorious.

Don't allow your thoughts to become strongholds of Satan.

Chapter 12: False Teachers

2nd Peter 2:2 *there will also be false teachers among you, who will secretly introduce destructive heresies*

Spiritual deception comes from a number of sources. Satan and his demons are the ultimate source of deception, but human beings are used to promote false ideas about God and the world. Jesus warned about false prophets[34] and said there would also be false christs.[35] Paul warned about false gospels.[36] And Peter warned believers about false prophets and false teachers.[37]

Peter describes the attributes of false teachers that we should examine and evaluate. He provides an important checklist we should consider when we hear others teach doctrine. We are called to discern truth from error. We should examine what we read and hear to see if it is true and aligns with Scripture.[38]

Peter talks about the work of false teachers. He says: "But false prophets also arose among the people, just as there will also be false teachers among you, who will secretly introduce destructive heresies, even denying the Master who bought them, bringing swift destruction upon themselves."[39] Notice that they were part of the church and "arose among the people." That means that in that day (and in our day) false teaching can come from those who are actually part of the church.

Peter also says that they "secretly introduce heresies." That doesn't mean that their teaching is secret. Often it is right out in the open. Instead, he means that there is a deceptive nature of their teaching. No false teacher announces that he or she is a false teacher. In fact, the false teacher might even have a large following and a media ministry.

He also calls their teaching "destructive heresies." False teachers are destructive because they tell lies about Jesus Christ and His work for us and in us. But the destruction is more than just spiritual. These heresies hurt people emotionally and financially. Lives can be destroyed. Heresy isn't harmless.

He also says that one element of these heresies is the fact that they deny the Master (the Lord Jesus Christ) who bought them. These false teachers appear to be saved even when they are not. This means that people who bring these destructive heresies can appear to be godly, and we should not be fooled by their fake piety.

Peter goes on to talk about the popularity of false teachers. He says: "Many will follow their sensuality, and because of them the way of the truth will be maligned."[40] False teachers may be very popular. Just because they are popular and just because some of their teaching works does not mean it is true. God's works will certainly bear fruit, but Satan can also counterfeit many things that God can do in our lives.

> *Many false teachers play to our selfish, sensual desires.*

He also talks about the sensuality of these teachers. Many false teachers play to our sensual desires or our desire to live for ourselves. And when they do so, they can often attract a crowd. But in the process, the truth is also maligned. This phrase could also be translated that the truth will be blasphemed. False teachers replace biblical teaching with erroneous, blasphemous teaching. Ultimately these teachers and their followers disgrace God and His honor.

Peter also talks about the strategy of false teachers. He says that: "in their greed they will exploit you with false words; their judgment from long ago is not idle, and their destruction is not asleep."[41] False teachers use greed (some translations say covetousness) to attract followers. While some are deceived through sensuality, others are deceived through greed and materialism. These false teachers present a gospel that has self-gratification at its heart.

False teachers use false words or deceptive words. The Greek word used here is the root for the word "plastic." Their words are fake or plastic. The false teachers are also able to exploit their followers. This could also be translated "make merchandise of." They use and manipulate their followers.

Peter also reminds us that their judgment is not idle. One day they will be judged for their heresy. Even though it may seem like they prosper, judgment is coming against them.

Essentially Peter is providing us with a three-part test we can use to evaluate what we read and hear. These tests help us discern whether someone is a false teacher. The first test is the <u>salvation test</u>. False teachers "introduce destructive heresies" that deny the salvation of Christ. The second test is the <u>truth test</u>. False teachers malign the truth of the gospel and entice their followers with sensuality. The third test is the <u>character test</u>. False teachers exploit their followers "with false words."

If we are to avoid spiritual deception, we need to watch out for false teachers. In subsequent chapters, we will consider the spiritual battle we are in and the spiritual armor we need to put on to defend ourselves.

> *False teachers fail the tests of 1) salvation, 2) the truth, and 3) character.*

Chapter 13: Spiritual Warfare

Ephesians 6:11 *Put on the full armor of God, so that you will be able to stand firm against the schemes of the devil.*

We are engaged in a spiritual battle that is often difficult for us to see because it takes place in the unseen, supernatural dimension. We may not be able to see it, but we can certainly feel its effects.

Paul understood the nature of spiritual warfare and provides this insight in his letter to the Ephesians:

> *Finally, be strong in the Lord and in the strength of His might. Put on the full armor of God, so that you will be able to stand firm against the schemes of the devil. For our struggle is not against flesh and blood, but against the rulers, against the powers, against the world forces of this darkness, against the spiritual forces of wickedness in the heavenly places. Therefore, take up the full armor of God, so that you will be able to resist in the evil day, and having done everything, to stand firm.*[42]

We are to be "strong in the Lord" and steadfast in our resistance to the Devil. One way we do this is to put on the whole armor of God (a topic we discuss in the next chapter). But before we put on the armor, we need to understand the nature of spiritual warfare.

In this passage, Paul not only assures us there is a spiritual war, but he also warns us that we must use the right weapons to fight the battle. These are divinely empowered weapons in order to repel Satan's attack. Our battle is not against flesh and blood but against spiritual forces.

From the day you became a Christian, you were already involved in spiritual warfare. But sadly, many Christians do not understand this. A spiritual battle is taking place around us and many are becoming spiritual casualties. Either they are mortally wounded in this spiritual battle or they have become spiritually weakened.

When Paul wrote to the church in Corinth he explained in more detail how we are to respond to this spiritual battle:

> *For though we walk in the flesh, we do not war according to the flesh, for the weapons of our warfare are not of the flesh, but divinely powerful for the destruction of fortresses. We are destroying speculations and every lofty thing raised up against the knowledge of God, and we are taking every thought captive to the obedience of Christ.*[43]

In a future chapter we will go into more detail about what Paul calls our walk, our weapons, and our warfare. For now, let's briefly examine how he describes spiritual warfare.

In the passage above, Paul says that though "we walk in the flesh, we do not war according to the flesh." In a previous chapter we talked about what it means to "walk in Christ." Here Paul reminds us that as we walk in Christ, we also engage in a war that is not an earthly one but a spiritual one. So even though we do walk in the flesh, our warfare is not fleshly.

Be willing to stand and fight the evil that threatens our world.

For the battle to be successful, we must be willing to stand up and fight. Many wars have been lost because good people refused to fight. The reason Satan has been so successful in the world is because Christians either have been unwilling to fight or have been unaware of the spiritual battle. We must be willing to stand and fight the evil that threatens our lives, our families, our communities, our nation, and our world.

Paul also teaches that "the weapons of our warfare are not of the flesh, but divinely powerful for the destruction of fortresses." One of the most important weapons of our warfare is the Word of God which Paul also calls the "Sword of the Spirit."[44] As we will discuss in the next chapter, we are not only to use the sword (the Bible) but we are also instructed to wear armor before we go into battle. We are to gird our loins with truth, wear the breastplate of righteousness and the helmet of salvation, and take up the shield of faith.

Finally, what is the goal of spiritual warfare? Paul says that we are destroying speculations and every lofty thing raised up against the knowledge of God, and we are taking every thought captive to the obedience of Christ." We cannot fight this war with physical weapons because our targets are not physical. They are intellectual and spiritual.

We must fight this spiritual battle with our heart, soul, spirit, and mind. These are spiritual targets that must be fought with spiritual weapons. And our ultimate goal is to pull down the strongholds of Satan in this world.

Can we be successful? In one of his other letters, Paul says we can have confidence because God "rescued us from the domain of darkness, and transferred us to the kingdom of His beloved Son, in whom we have redemption, the forgiveness of sins."[45]

We cannot fight this war with physical weapons. These spiritual targets must be fought with spiritual weapons.

Chapter 14: Armor of God

Ephesians 6:14 *Stand firm therefore, having girded your loins with truth*

The comic book superhero, Iron Man, first appeared in Marvel Comics back in the 1960s. Since then a number of films have been made about this fictional billionaire playboy, Tony Stark, who created a powerful suit of armor giving him the ability to fight crime, fight terrorists, and protect the world. His success was due to his armor and other technological devices integrated into his suit.

Iron Man may be fictional, but our spiritual armor is real and necessary. Anyone who goes into battle needs armor, so Paul admonishes us to "put on the full armor of God."[46] He also reminds us who the enemy is. "For our struggle is not against flesh and blood, but against the rulers, against the powers, against the world forces of this darkness, against the spiritual forces of wickedness in the heavenly places."[47] Our enemy is Satan and his demons.

Paul uses the imagery of armor to describe what we need as Christians to defend ourselves. He spent long periods in prison and saw the armor of the Roman soldiers who guarded him. When he talks about armor, weapons, and warfare he is helping us understand the spiritual battle around us.

He describes six types of armor that are divided into two groups. The first three are those we already have. The second three are those we are to take up. In other words, we wear the first three and then are to pick up the second three each day just as a soldier going into battle will pick up the armor he needs for battle.

> *Stand firm therefore, having girded your loins with truth, and having put on the breastplate of righteousness, and having shod your feet with the preparation of the gospel*

of peace; in addition to all, taking up the shield of faith with which you will be able to extinguish all the flaming arrows of the evil one. And take the helmet of salvation, and the sword of the Spirit, which is the word of God.[48]

Let's look at each of these six pieces of armor and see if we can discover the spiritual significance of each of them.

1. The belt: "having girded your loins with truth." In order to fight, a Roman soldier would gird up his tunic by tucking the ends into his belt. The belt on a Roman soldier was made of leather and metal and protected the body of the soldier. The sword was carried on the belt. And the breastplate was attached to the belt. So the belt was an important piece of armor because of how it helped the Roman soldier to fight.

   Likewise, truth is important in our dealing with spiritual warfare. A discerning Christian must be able to handle the "word of truth"[49] and expose Satan's lies.

   Be able to handle the truth and expose Satan's lies.

2. The breastplate: We also have "the breastplate of righteousness." The soldier wore a protective vest made of leather often overlaid with metal. It protected his upper body and heart from flying arrows or strikes from a sword. Our righteousness comes not from ourselves but from Christ's righteousness placed upon us. His righteousness protects us from the intrusion of Satan and his demons in our lives. Essentially, it protects our hearts.

3. The shoes: "and having shod your feet with the preparation of the gospel of peace." The gospel is the message that we are to bring to the world. Often a Roman soldier's shoes would have spikes allowing him to "stand firm." Three times in this passage, Paul admonishes us "to stand firm."

It is important for us to have such protection. Every day we are walking in enemy territory.

4. The shield: We are to take "the shield of faith with which you will be able to extinguish all the flaming arrows of the evil one." When Roman soldiers stood shoulder to shoulder, their large shields would provide an almost impenetrable barrier. Likewise, our "shield of faith" protects us from any arrows Satan might launch at us. We cannot prevent Satan from sending these arrows, but the shield of faith can protect us from them.

5. The helmet: We are also to "take the helmet of salvation." The helmet protected the soldier's head from blows. It absorbed the shock of these blows and allowed him to continue to fight. Likewise, the helmet of salvation allows us to absorb the mental attacks from Satan knowing that we are living in eternity.

6. The sword: We are also to take up "the sword of the Spirit, which is the word of God." Every soldier needs a weapon with which to destroy and take captive the enemy. We use the Bible like Jesus did against Satan's temptation.[50] Likewise, we are to use the Bible to ward off temptation and achieve victory. It is without error containing everything needed for life and godliness.[51] If you aren't convinced of this, the rest of the armor will not be effective.

We can be victorious in the midst of a spiritual battle. We cannot be passive and make no effort to change because that will not bring victory.[52] And we cannot win on our own efforts and self-discipline.[53] We must depend on the armor of God.

We can only be victorious through depending on the armor of God.

Chapter 15: What do Christians Believe?

Revelation 3:16-17 *So, because you are lukewarm, and neither hot nor cold, I will spit you out of my mouth. For you say, I am rich, I have prospered, and I need nothing, not realizing that you are wretched, pitiable, poor, blind, and naked.*

Do born-again Christians have a biblical worldview? Back in the 1960s, Harry Blamires (a British theologian, novelist, and literary critic) wrote a book entitled, *The Christian Mind: How Should a Christian Think.* His conclusion even back then was that: "There is no longer a Christian mind."[1] Jesus said that we are to love God with all our heart, soul, and mind.[2] Apparently we have not loved God with our minds for many decades.

More recently, author Nancy Pearcey says in her book (*Total Truth: Liberating Christianity from Its Cultural Captivity*) that we have a sacred-secular split in our lives.[3] Our spiritual lives are cordoned off to personal, private lives of religious values. Our faith does not intersect with the secular, public sector where facts (not values) hold sway.

Christian Smith in *Souls in Transition* charted the spiritual lives of thousands of teenagers for five years.[4] He documented many of the trends of this group of "emerging adults." One of most shocking was our analysis that concluded that out of 2550 people he was able to interview after five years, only one had a consistent set of biblical beliefs and practices.

Some have said that these emerging adults treat religious beliefs like items in a cafeteria. They pick and choose what sounds good and suits their needs and lifestyles. They seem less concerned about whether their beliefs are consistent and coherent.

Another disturbing trend among emerging adults is that while those professing to be born-again have dropped by 25% from 1990, those professing no religious affiliation have increased by a factor of three over the same time period. These results mean that today less than 20% are born-again while over 30% profess no religious affiliation.[5]

Probe Ministries commissioned the Barna Group to do an extensive survey of born-again adults between the ages of 18 and 40.[6] We did this to get a better picture of the spiritual lives of those who are and/or will be parents of our next generation and who will most likely be the future leaders of our churches.

Previous studies by the Barna Group document that about one-third (35%) of 18-to-40-year-old Americans are born-again. This means they agreed that they had an ongoing personal relationship with Jesus Christ and that they are going to heaven because their sins are forgiven and have accepted Jesus Christ as their Savior. Using Census data, we can assume that there are about 34 million born-again Americans in that age range.

Fewer than 1 in 10 young Americans have a biblical worldview.

Our research found that of these born-again Christians, one-third had a biblical worldview. That means they had orthodox views on six questions about God, Jesus, salvation, morality, Satan and the Bible. Thus, about 10 million 18-to-40-year-olds have a biblical worldview.

However, when this group of born-again Christians with a biblical worldview was asked six additional questions, the numbers dropped once again. These six questions were about the uniqueness of Jesus, science, sharing their faith, world religions, their purpose in life, and the accuracy of the Bible. Only half of these born-again Christians with a biblical worldview could answer these questions consistent with the Bible. This amounts to about 5 percent of the total population of 18-to-40-year-olds.

The survey also showed that a biblical worldview impacts our daily lives. We asked about various ways these 18-to-40-

year-olds engaged their faith. Those with a biblical worldview practiced their faith at higher levels. When we combined those who prayed, went to church, studied their Bible, and attended a small group, those with a biblical worldview were almost twice as likely (44% to 24%) as those without a biblical worldview.

We also found that very few of the born-again Christians we surveyed shared their faith. Only 3 percent witnessed to someone in a typical month, and none of those that said they did so were in the group that had a consistent biblical worldview and biblical practices.

Extrapolating these percentages over the coming decades, we see ominous implications for the future of the Christian church and ministries. Cultural captivity isn't just an abstract theological idea. It will affect churches, missions, and Christian organizations. It will affect everything from the future stability of these organizations to their participation in evangelism. If these trends don't change, then many churches and Christian organizations won't be here decades from now. And if they do survive, they certainly won't be as vibrant as they are today.

It is one thing to gather statistics and lament that so many are culturally captive. It is quite another to do something about it. This book and the materials associated with it are an attempt to reverse some of these disturbing trends. Our goal is to encourage the church to free the minds of cultural captives and build them into confident ambassadors for Christ. We encourage you to consider areas where you may be captive and look at how you can encourage others you know to live as free people in Christ.

Fewer than 3% of born-again, young adults combine a biblical worldview with cultural beliefs.

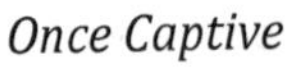

Chapter 16: Naturalism

Colossians 2:8 *See to it that no one takes you captive through philosophy and empty deception, according to the tradition of men, according to the elementary principles of the world, rather than according to Christ.*

Our theme verse, Colossians 2:8, has the only occurrence of the word "philosophy" in the Bible. Our philosophy or worldview is the way in which we try to explain how the world works. Everyone has a worldview, and everyone is affected in one way or another by the various philosophies of the world. Paul describes four specific ways that our thinking can be taken captive by the philosophy of the world. In this chapter and beyond, we are going to look at some of these philosophies and the impact they are having on us and the world around us.

One dominant philosophy of our world is *naturalism*. It is the belief that only natural laws and forces operate in the world. A naturalistic view rejects the supernatural and believes nothing exists beyond the natural world. Although naturalism existed before Charles Darwin, the theory of evolution provided an intellectual foundation for naturalism. Darwinian evolution assumes the world resulted from strictly natural processes of random mutations and natural selection. No Divine intervention, say the evolutionists, was necessary for the diversity and complexity of life on this planet.

A naturalistic view of knowledge therefore assumes that religious ideas and philosophical absolutes are not true. And if Darwinian evolution is true, then those ideas and absolutes are not true. Concepts like truth, honesty, integrity, and morality are fraudulent ideas and concepts. They are merely symbolic but not true in any real sense.

How powerful is Darwinism? One atheist refers to it as a "universal acid." This is an allusion to a children's riddle about an acid that is so corrosive that it eats through everything including the flask that holds it. In other words, Darwinism is too corrosive to be contained. It eats through every academic field destroying ethics, morality, truth, and absolutes. When finished, Darwinism "eats through almost every traditional concept and leaves in its wake a revolutionized worldview."[7]

Atheists certainly understand the impact of a philosophy like naturalism based upon the theory of evolution. Yet, many Christians embrace naturalism and evolution and merely incorporate it into their worldview without considering the impact this worldly philosophy will have on them. Naturalism does not have good answers for such issues as the origin of life, the origin of diversity, and the incredible complexity of life forms. Moreover, the secular philosophy of naturalism makes no room for God, the Bible, and spiritual matters.

We shouldn't put our faith beneath the elementary principles of evolution or the philosophy of naturalism. Nevertheless, many Christians are taken captive by accepting a secular philosophy as part of their worldview.

Don't put Christianity beneath the elementary principles of evolution.

What is the difference if we adopt a secular view of the world? In the case of naturalism, it affects your self-worth and human dignity. Evolutionist George Gaylord Simpson said: "Man is the result of a purposeless and natural process that did not have him in mind."[8] If evolution is true, then you have no significance or dignity. You are merely a cosmic accident.

The Bible does not say you are an accident. David, reflecting on God's omnipresence, was overwhelmed by the fact that God's care for him began while he was still in his mother's womb.

For You formed my inward parts; You wove me in my mother's womb. I will give thanks to You, for I am fearfully and wonderfully made; Wonderful are Your

> *works, And my soul knows it very well. My frame was not hidden from You, When I was made in secret, And skillfully wrought in the depths of the earth; Your eyes have seen my unformed substance; And in Your book were all written, The days that were ordained for me, When as yet there was not one of them.*[9]

God determined who you were and determined your gifts, talents, and abilities. He determined so many aspects of your life. He planned your birth, your death, and "the days that were ordained" for you.[10] He even determined your race, nationality, and time and place where you will live. The Bible says, "He made from one man every nation of mankind to live on all the face of the earth, having determined their appointed times and the boundaries of their habitation."[11]

Evolution teaches that you are the result of a purposeless process. Essentially you are an accident. The Bible teaches there is a plan and purpose to your life created by God. Paul reminds us that Christ "is the image of the invisible God, the firstborn of all creation. For by Him all things were created, both in the heavens and on earth, visible and invisible, whether thrones or dominions or rulers or authorities—all things have been created through Him and for Him. He is before all things, and in Him all things hold together."[12]

An important step in ridding ourselves of cultural captivity is rejecting the secular view of naturalism and embracing the fact that God exists and is the creator of the world around us. Remember Jesus Christ is the head of all creation and He has a plan for you because you are not an accident.

You are not an accident.
God has a plan and a purpose for your life.

Chapter 17: Legalism

Colossians 2:16-17 *No one is to act as your judge in regard to food or drink or in respect to a festival or a new moon or a Sabbath day—things which are a mere shadow of what is to come; but the substance belongs to Christ.*

Another philosophy that leads to cultural captivity is legalism. In the verse above, Paul warned them about those in their midst who were taking them captive through the subtle lies of legalism. These false teachers would commend the good start of these Gentile Christians, but then challenge them to now follow the Old Testament laws in order to become righteous before God.

You might notice that what is listed in these verses are not instructions on purity or righteousness. Rather they are specific Old Testament practices that were given to Israel before the coming of Christ. The Passover is a foreshadowing of Christ's sacrifice as the Lamb of God. While the deliverance of Israel is significant, consider how much more significant is Christ's death which provides us with deliverance from the slavery of sin and separation from God. The previous feasts and festivals are no longer necessary now that we have Christ in our lives.

Jesus addressed legalism among the Pharisees and scribes. They established all sorts of rules and regulations that were binding on all Jews. Starting with the Law (which included the five books of Moses, the Ten Commandments, and other parts of the Old Testament), they set out to compile the various oral traditions and even began to develop interpretations of these laws. In the end, they even had interpretations of the interpretations collected in numerous volumes.

By the time of Christ, the Pharisees and the scribes were actually following the traditions of men rather than the law of God. Jesus pointedly asked them, "why do you break the commandment of God for the sake of your tradition?"[13] Jesus also condemned the Pharisees by saying, "you also outwardly appear righteous to men, but inside you are full of hypocrisy and lawlessness."[14] Jesus therefore accused them, on numerous occasions, of being hypocrites.[15]

Legalism is our attempt to produce righteousness apart from God. We are challenged to follow additional rules and regulations that we believe will merit favor before God. But in the end, these unbiblical rules bind us and drain the joy from our lives.

When we give people an ever expanding "to-do list" that is uncoupled from God's power, we wear people down and ultimately drive people away from the gospel. Paul warned Timothy that in the last days there would be people "having a form of godliness but denying its power."[16] He counsels him to avoid such people.

Our churches provide a long list of things to do: be righteous, be a better spouse, be a good steward, be a good witness, dress modestly, avoid addictions, avoid entanglements with the world. And the world adds to this list: be green, end hunger, help the poor, be a good citizen, be compassionate and tolerant. While these are good lists, they will merely wear us down if we try to do all of them in the flesh uncoupled from God's power.

Legalism says we can be righteous by our own effort.

The danger of legalism is the belief that we can do all of this in the flesh and yet be righteous. Isaiah says that "All of us have become like one who is unclean, and all our righteous acts are like filthy rags"[17]

Another danger of legalism is that is drives people away from the gospel. The unbeliever assumes that he or she must do all these activities and be a particular type of person in order to be a Christian. And Christians in a church dominated by legalism finally give up and leave the church angry and exhausted.

Legalism also leads to church splits. Christians become preoccupied with intramural wars over liturgy, worship music, and church practice. This not only hurts the body of Christ but drives unbelievers away from the gospel.

Another form of legalism is the practice of picking and choosing only the parts of God's truth that you feel is applicable to you. Jesus condemned the Pharisees for doing this when they committed their resources to God so they would not have to help their mother or father.[18]

We see that today as well. One national survey of youth (18-to-23-year-olds) found that a majority (51%) of them said: "it is okay to pick and choose their religious beliefs without having to accept the teachings of their religious faith as a whole."[19] We are not to pick and choose our beliefs but to follow biblical precepts and principles, neither adding nor subtracting from them.

The answer to legalism is to realize that as Paul teaches, we no longer live under the law, but instead live under grace.[20] The Bible teaches that God "made the world and all things in it, since He is Lord of heaven and earth, does not dwell in temples made with hands."[21] We are free in Christ[22] and no longer bound by the law or by man-made rules and regulations.

We can never be good enough.
Only through God's grace can we be redeemed.

Chapter 18: Mysticism

Colossians 2:18 *Let no one keep defrauding you of your prize by delighting in self-abasement and worship of angels*

Mysticism is another philosophy that leads to cultural captivity. When Paul wrote to the Colossians, he warned them about false teachers who would attempt to seduce them into mystical ideas.

> *"Let no one keep defrauding you of your prize by delighting in self-abasement and the worship of the angels, taking his stand on visions he has seen, inflated without cause by his fleshly mind, and not holding fast to the head, from whom the entire body, being supplied and held together by the joints and ligaments, grows with a growth which is from God."*[23]

The word mysticism comes from the Greek word for the mystery religions that existed at the time Paul was writing to these Christians. He is describing someone who is "taking his stand on visions he has seen." In other words, this is a person who has had some vision and is mixing that vision with the revelation of Scripture.

At the time Paul was writing to a church that was a mixture of Jews and Gentiles. Many were young Christians and may have brought their pagan ideas into the church. This would include the idea that you receive spiritual revelations by entering into an ecstatic state. These Christians also lived in a culture where many claimed they were receiving visions from the gods. If these young Christians did not have discernment, they might actually believe that someone who has these visions was spiritually superior to them. After all, some of the apostles had visions, so it would be easy for the undiscerning to confuse these pagan visions (which most likely had a demonic source) with God's revelation.

Mysticism has been a major area of cultural captivity both in church history and even in our present day. We see in Paul's letter to the church in Corinth, that believers were confused about speaking in tongues and other spiritual manifestations. Some of the believers were essentially "babes in Christ" who could not handle the solid food of God's word. He reminded them that when they were pagans, they had been led astray.[24] Because of their previous exposure to paganism, they were vulnerable to false doctrine.

Throughout church history, certain churches and denominations have brought mystical rituals and practices into their worship experience. They may take the form of chants, icons, or prescribed practices not found in Scripture but part of a tradition that borrows heavily from mystical ideas. And many of these practices are found today not only in North American churches but in churches in other parts of the world.

Mysticism is quite prevalent outside of the church and can have a strong cultural influence on Christians. Many of the books on the best-seller lists over the last few decades dealing with spirituality are not books that promote biblical Christianity but rather books that promote an Eastern philosophy of religion or the New Age Movement.

> ***Many popular books promote mystic religion under a guise of Christianity.***

In *The Secret*, Rhonda Byrne teaches "the Law of Attraction."[25] She believes that thoughts become things. So if you think hard enough about something, it will take place. She believes we create our own circumstances and therefore can change our circumstances with our thoughts.

Eckhardt Tolle, author of *A New Earth: Awakening to Your Life's Purpose*, teaches a version of Eastern mysticism which he discovered in a vision.[26] He teaches that we are all part of the universal life force to which we should desire to return. He misquotes Jesus through his book and actually identifies Him as one of the early proponents of this mystic religion. Nevertheless, millions have purchased books by Eckhardt Tolle, and many of these people are people who attend church on a regular basis.

Most of these mystical religions and philosophies teach that Jesus was not the son of God but rather a prophet or enlightened person showing us the way. Proponents of these mystical ideas teach that Buddha, Krishna, and Jesus are all trying to communicate the same truth in different ways.

These ideas have certainly taken root in America. One survey of emerging adults (18-to-23-year-olds) found that over 70 percent rejected the idea that only one religion is true.[27] The Probe Ministries survey of born-again young adults found that less than half believe Jesus Christ is the only way to heaven.[95]

Christians can become culturally captive in many ways. Mysticism seems to be a growing threat to orthodox beliefs in God, Jesus, and the Bible. We should base our faith on the solid rock of God's word and the solid food it provides[28] not on the mystical teachings being promoted in our world today.

Mystical thought teaches many ways to God.
Jesus Christ taught He was the only way to the Father.

Chapter 19: Asceticism

Colossians 2:23 *These are matters which have, to be sure, the appearance of wisdom in self-made religion and self-abasement and severe treatment of the body, but are of no value against fleshly indulgence.*

In his letter to the Colossians, Paul warns them about the danger of asceticism. In the last chapter, we saw his warning about those who delighted in "self-abasement."[29] He continues in the following verses to explain why this should be a concern to Christians.

"If you have died with Christ to the elementary principles of the world, why, as if you were living in the world, do you submit yourself to decrees, such as, "Do not handle, do not taste, do not touch!" (which all refer to things destined to perish with use)—in accordance with the commandments and teachings of men? These are matters which have, to be sure, the appearance of wisdom in self-made religion and self-abasement and severe treatment of the body, but are of no value against fleshly indulgence."[30]

Asceticism is the belief that we need to live a life of extreme self-denial or self-abasement in order to release our soul from bondage in our body. This philosophy was found among the Jews (the Essenes) and among the Greeks (Stoics) at the time when Paul was writing to the Colossians.

Some of the false teachers of that day promoted the idea that since human beings are material, they cannot approach God because He is spirit. So they taught that in order to reach to God, you had to go through various spiritual entities that moved you from the human plane of existence to the Divine plane of existence. They saw angels as these intermediaries. That explains why many of them worshipped angels. It also explains why they rejected the idea that Jesus Christ was both God and man. They reasoned that if the material body is bad and the immaterial soul is good, then God would not take on the body of a man.

The foundation of asceticism is self-denial. But we should ask, Is it wrong to deny yourself? No. That is what Jesus called for us to do as His disciples. He said: *"If anyone wishes to come after Me, he must deny himself, and take up his cross daily and follow Me. For whoever wishes to save his life will lose it, but whoever loses his life for My sake, he is the one who will save it."*[31] But asceticism is based upon a false assumption that our material body is bad and that we can only reach to God by our good works and self-denial. The Bible, however, teaches that all of our good works "are like filthy rags."[32] We are not saved by our good works. Instead, the Bible teaches that by grace we are saved by faith, not as a result of works.[33]

Asceticism is based on a false assumption – our material body is bad and must be denied.

We are not to worship angels. We are only to worship God.[34] This is an important biblical principle to remember as we live in a culture that promotes false views about angels (in television and the movies) and even encourages an unhealthy interest in angels.

Paul says that even if "an angel from heaven, should preach to you a gospel contrary to what we have preached to you, he is to be accursed."[35] We are not to seek contact with angels nor should we use them to approach God. There is only one mediator between God and man, and that is Jesus Christ.[36]

In these last few chapters we have discussed four types of false teaching that had the potential to take Christians captive in the first century. They also have the power and influence to do that today. The first step in preventing cultural captivity is recognizing these forms of captivity as we have done in these last few chapters.

We should also ask ourselves why we would want to add anything to our Christian faith that is not sanctioned in the Bible. Paul reminds us in his letter to the Colossians that we are already complete in Christ.[37] How can any of these false teachings add anything to the fullness we have in Jesus Christ? We should reject these false philosophies and empty deception.[38] Instead, we should "walk in Him."[39]

These false teachings do not add to the work of Christ; rather they subtract from it.

9/29

Chapter 20: Truth

John 14:6 *I am the way, and the truth, and the life; no one comes to the Father but through Me.*

We live in a world with many definitions of truth. Most of us have had someone say, "You have your view of truth, and I have my view of truth." Some in society will state dogmatically there is no such thing as truth. And in the Bible, Pilate asks the famous question: "What is truth?"[40]

Not so long ago, people tended to believe in truth with a capital "T" based upon a belief in God or at least based upon a belief there were some moral absolutes. Today, a greater number of people in society believe in truth with a small "t." This idea that everyone has their own personal truth is one example of pluralism (a topic we will discuss in the next chapter).

To understand this changed view of truth, we might consider the story of three baseball umpires. In their book, *Truth is Stranger Than It Used to Be*, the authors have us imagine three umpires meeting after a day at the ballpark.[41] As they reflect on the day's activities, one umpire declares, "There's balls and there's strikes, and I call 'em the way they are." Another responds, "There's balls and there's strikes, and I call 'em the way I see 'em." And the third umpire said, "There's balls and there's strikes, and they ain't nothing until I call them."

Each of the umpires might make the same call, but they are making it for very different reasons. The first umpire believes that balls and strikes exist in reality. The second believes he can perceive them correctly. The last umpire doesn't believe they exist until he declares what they are.

These three different views of balls and strikes correspond with three different views of truth. The first is what we might call *premodernism*. This is a God-centered view of the universe that believes in divine revelation. Most of the ancient world had this view of true and believed that truth is absolute ("I call 'em the way they are").

By the time of the Enlightenment, Western culture was moving into a time of *modernism*. This view, which matured in the last century, was influenced by the scientific revolution, and began to reject a belief in God. In this modern world, people are less likely to see truth as absolute and instead tend to believe truth is relative to the observer ("I call 'em the way I see 'em").

A prominent perspective on truth today is what many call *postmodernism*. In this view, there is a complete loss of hope for truth. Truth is not discovered; truth is created ("they ain't nothing until I call them"). Postmodernism is built upon the belief that truth doesn't exist except as the individual wants it to exist. Truth isn't objective or absolute. Truth is personal and relative.

In today's world, truth is not absolute, but rather a social construct.

What are some of the themes that postmodernists have written about? The first is the theory that truth is a social construct. In other words, there is no absolute truth. The ideas we think are universally true are merely ideas that powerful people and groups use to manipulate others. Thus, postmodernists reject assertions from anyone who claims to know something that is true for everyone, everywhere, at any time. One can easily see that a Christian worldview conflicts with a postmodern view of the world.

Another postmodern theme is the rejection of the confidence modernism has about the world. The modern scientist assumes there is an objective reality (like the umpire who "calls 'em the way that they are"). The postmodernist believes that truth is not objective but subjective. Because they believe that truth is subjective, they are skeptical of ever being able to arrive at an absolute truth.

As Christians we should reject the confidence of modernism and the pessimism of postmodernism. Modernism is too dependent on science as the only valid source of truth and does not consider that we are fallen people in a fallen world.[42] Postmodernism leaves us with no hope of knowing what is real and true.

As Christians, we begin with first principles concerning Jesus and truth. Jesus said, "I am the way, and the truth, and the life; no one comes to the Father but through Me."[43] Jesus spoke the truth with authority. The Bible records that: "When Jesus had finished these words, the crowds were amazed at His teaching; for He was teaching them as one having authority, and not as their scribes."[44] When Jesus confronted the Pharisees He reminded them that He spoke the truth: "But because I speak the truth, you do not believe Me. 'Which one of you convicts Me of sin? If I speak truth, why do you not believe Me?'"[45] And Paul writing to Christians reminded them as a believer that "truth is in Jesus."[46]

The Christian's confidence in truth does not rest upon the confidence of modernism and the scientific method nor in the pessimism of postmodernism which believes truth is merely a social construct. Our confidence is in the person of Jesus Christ who was and is truth.

As God, Jesus Christ defines absolute truth.

Chapter 21: Pluralism

Acts 4:11-12 *This Jesus is the stone that was rejected by you, the builders, which has become the cornerstone. And there is* ***salvation in no one else****, for there is no other name under heaven given among men by which we must be saved.*

In the verses above, Peter clearly states Jesus is the only way by which we must be saved. But, in this pluralistic society we confront a multitude of competing views on ethics and religion. Many different approaches are assumed to result in eternal life.

Perhaps you have heard an old joke that starts with something like: "There was a Jewish rabbi, a Catholic priest, and a Baptist pastor sitting in a boat fishing." Lots of jokes that start out that way and end with different punch lines. Today, however, if we wanted to be inclusive we would also have to add a Muslim imam, a Buddhist monk, a Hindu devotee, a New Age spiritualist, a Wiccan witch, and an atheist or agnostic. The joke would be too long, and the boat may not be big enough.

This is the pluralistic world of the 21st century. It has been estimated that there are about 30,000 different religious groups just in North America. If we focus on groups having at least 2,000 members, we still have about 1,600 different religious groups.[47] Although these numbers are large, remember Christianity was born in a pluralistic culture. There were Jews who worshipped Yahweh and rejected Jesus as the Messiah. The Greeks and Romans worshiped a pantheon of gods and rejected Jesus as part of the one true God. Other foreign religions also proclaimed various religious ideas in conflict with Christianity.

Over the centuries, Christians have responded to the challenge of religious pluralism in different ways. Some have rejected these other religions, while others decided to believe that these other religions might be valid ways to approach God.

One popular view in society is varying religions merely say things differently, but they all teach the same basic truth. Steve Turner pokes fun at this idea when he says: "We believe that all religions are basically the same, at least the one we read was. They all believe in love and goodness. They only differ on matters of creation, sin, heaven, hell, God, and salvation."[48]

Contrary to popular belief, all religions do not teach the same thing and cannot all be true. Either God exists or God does not exist. If God exists, the religions of the world may be true, but by definition atheism is false. If God is personal, then the theistic religions that teach that God is personal (Judaism, Christianity, and Islam) could be true, but eastern religions that teach an impersonal God (Hinduism, Buddhism) would be false. Either Jesus is the Messiah or not. If Jesus is the Messiah then Christianity is true, but Judaism and Islam are false.

The belief that all religions lead to God is called inclusivism, and that all people will be saved by God is called universalism. These are popular today because of our society's emphasis on tolerance and universal acceptance of nearly every view and perspective. Often you will hear the statement: "It doesn't really matter what you believe, as long as you are sincere."

You can sincerely believe in a false religion and be sincerely wrong.

Sadly, sincerity is overrated in our society. You can sincerely eat a poisonous mushroom thinking you are safe. You can sincerely believe that you can fly off a building and not be subject to the laws of gravity. You can sincerely believe in a false religion. People who are sincere can also be sincerely wrong.

The opposite of inclusivism is exclusivism. This is the view that not all religions are true and not all religions lead to God. Jesus taught this saying: "I am the way, and the truth, and the life; no one comes to the Father but through Me."[49] If this teaching by Jesus is true, then by definition other religions are false. There are not many ways to God; only one.

If there were many ways to God, why did Jesus Christ go through the extreme sacrifice on the cross? If there was any other way, He would not have had to die just to provide another way. He would only do it if that was the only way possible.

Christ's exclusive claim is hard for many in society to accept because we live in a pluralistic culture. "How can Christianity be true," they ask, "and all other religions be false?" As noted previously, over 70 percent of emerging adults rejected the idea that only one religion is true.[50] Similarly, among born-again young adults less than half believe Jesus Christ is the only way to heaven.[95] Although the teaching by Jesus is eternally true, many in our society reject it because we are surrounded by so many other religions and religious groups.

Salvation in Christ is based upon the foundational truth that He is the way, and the truth, and the life and that salvation only comes through Him. This may be a difficult belief to accept in a pluralistic society, but it is foundational to our faith. We should not be arrogant or mean-spirited. Instead we should be humble, loving, and gracious. Peter reminds us that: "The Lord is not slow about His promise, as some count slowness, but is patient toward you, not wishing for any to perish but for all to come to repentance."[51] God wants all people to be saved.

Christ's exclusive claim of salvation should never be used as an exclusive weapon against others. All of us have sinned and are sinners.[52] Christians who have accepted the gospel of Jesus Christ have been saved by grace.[53] This is the good news that we must share with those in the pluralistic society that erroneously believes that there are many paths to God.

Christ's exclusivity is not a weapon, but a gift.

Chapter 22: What Do Christians Accept?

Romans 12:2 *And do not be conformed to this world, but be transformed by the renewing of your mind, so that you may prove what the will of God is, that which is good, acceptable and perfect.*

The false views of the world affect what we believe and how we behave. If we are not using a biblical standard to evaluate the ideas and trends around us, we are likely to accept false ideas and live a life contrary to the Bible. The world seduces us to live in ways that negate our testimony of eternal life in Christ.

Paul was certainly concerned that worldly thinking would result in false ideas and false living. As he points out in Romans 12:2 (above), we should not be conformed to this world and the ideas and living standards of the world. Instead, we should transform our minds with biblical truth.

On a number of occasions in his letters to Christians and churches, Paul warned them not to fall into the sins of the world. To the Colossians he said: "*Therefore consider the members of your earthly body as dead to immorality, impurity, passion, evil desire, and greed, which amounts to idolatry. For it is because of these things that the wrath of God will come upon the sons of disobedience, and in them you also once walked, when you were living in them. But now you also, put them all aside: anger, wrath, malice, slander, and abusive speech from your mouth.*"[1]

Paul reminds them since their bodies are dead to sin and worldly influence, they should subdue carnal and evil attitudes and actions. He also acknowledges that they once walked in these sins. But now that they are saved and walking in Christ, they must put aside that behavior and no longer indulge in it.

When he writes to the church in Corinth, Paul makes a similar statement. "*Or do you not know that the unrighteous will not inherit the kingdom of God? Do not be deceived; neither fornicators, nor idolaters, nor adulterers, nor effeminate, nor homosexuals, nor thieves, nor the covetous, nor drunkards, nor revilers, nor swindlers, will inherit the kingdom of God. Such were some of you; but you were washed, but you were sanctified, but you were justified in the name of the Lord Jesus Christ and in the Spirit of our God."*[2]

Paul is warning them against the great evils that were formerly part of their lives. In other passages, he acknowledges the pull these sins can still have on a Christian. But he reminds them of their conversion and the change it brought about ("such were some of you") in their lives. He tells them not to be deceived into believing that they can sow to the flesh and yet reap everlasting life. Believers should live the Christian life and their testimony should be different from the world.

You cannot sow to the flesh and reap eternity.

That isn't what we find. Born-again Christians aren't always thinking like Christians and are often willing to accept the world's ideas. And as we will see in the next chapter, born-again Christians aren't always living a consistent Christian life.

In earlier chapters, we referred to a study Probe Ministries commissioned through the Barna Group. This extensive survey of born-again, young adults gives us a perspective on the thoughts and actions of those who are and will be parents of our next generation and who will most likely be the future leaders of our churches.

When those surveyed were asked to pick the statement that most closely described their ultimate purpose in life, more than half (54%) said it was to "serve God and live out His will for my life." A much higher percentage (70%) of those with a biblical worldview picked this compared with those (47%) without a biblical worldview. Other statements that were picked included: "be a good person" and "live life to the fullest" and "marry, have family, raise loving, productive children."[3]

While there is nothing wrong with a Christian wanting to be a good person or wanting to raise a good family, we should nevertheless be disturbed that only about half of those surveyed picked as their *ultimate* purpose in life to serve God and live for Him. Even if you add in some of the other choices on the survey that might be considered as spiritually engaging (e.g., "praise and glorify God" or "lead others to salvation"), we are still left with a significant percentage of Christians who define their purpose in life more in worldly terms than biblical terms.

When asked how they go about making decisions regarding moral and ethical choices, there were also differences between those who had a biblical worldview and those who did not. A much higher percentage (82%) of Christians with a biblical worldview follow a set of principles or standards regarding moral and ethical choices in their personal life than Christians (50%) without a biblical worldview. The survey also found similar differences when asking about how Christians make moral and ethical choices regarding work or public life.[4]

For Christians, the Bible should be our source of truth. Born-again adults with a biblical worldview were much more likely (95%) to identify the Bible as a source of truth than born-again Christians without a biblical worldview (59%).[5]

The survey also found a strong correlation with behavior. For example, active church goers are much more likely (83%) to identify the Bible as a source of truth than non-active churchgoers (49%). Also, adults who are cohabiting are much less likely to identify the Bible as a source of truth. This statistic reminds us of the correlation between what Christians accept and what Christians do. We will look at the relationship between beliefs and behaviors in the next chapter.

Our decision making is often inconsistent with a biblical worldview.

Chapter 23: What Do Christians Do?

1st Corinthians 6:18 *Flee from sexual immorality. Every other sin a person commits is outside the body, but the sexually immoral person sins against his own body.*

If we are not thinking biblically, then we are probably not acting biblically. False ideas impact our beliefs and our actions. In essence, the world shoves us into its mold unless we consciously resist those cultural pressures with a biblical worldview. This is why Paul warned believers not to "be conformed to this world."[6] He understood the forces in the world that cause us to believe and act contrary to God's word. When the world influences us in this way, our testimony to the world is also affected. The unbeliever looks at the Christian and doesn't see any difference between Christian behavior and worldly behavior.

We should not only believe biblical truths but live them out before the watching world. Peter encourages Christians to keep their behavior *"excellent among the Gentiles, so that in the thing in which they slander you as evildoers, they may because of your good deeds, as they observe them, glorify God in the day of visitation."*[7] If Christians live a godly life, it will be distinctive and call attention to the truthfulness of the gospel.

The Probe Ministries study of born-again, young adults discovered struggles with many issues.[8] Nearly half of these born-again adults admit they are challenged by impatience and anger. Many struggle with judging others, cursing, and anxiety. Approximately one third of these adults grapple with losing their temper, gossiping, lust, or succumbing to negativity.

Anger, impatience, and cursing showed up in a number of ways in the survey. James reminds us that *"the anger of man does not achieve the righteousness of God."*[9] Paul commanded the Ephesians: *"Be angry, and yet do not sin; do not let the sun go down on your anger."*[10] Instead, he says, we are to speak the truth in love and use our words to build up others, and not allow destructive words to pour from our lips.[11]

Other areas in which more than one out of five born-again adults "miss the mark" include: selfishness, not attending church, pride, jealousy, coveting, unforgiveness, and lying.

The unbeliever looks at Christians and does not detect any difference in behavior.

A number of born-again adults admitted to some form of sexual sin. This included sex outside of marriage, pornography, adultery, and same-sex attraction. Not surprisingly those with a biblical worldview were less likely to be involved in a sexual sin than those without a biblical worldview.

Paul commands that we: "*Flee immorality. Every other sin that a man commits is outside the body.*"[12] He also says: "*For this is the will of God, your sanctification; that is, that you abstain from sexual immorality; that each of you know how to possess his own vessel in sanctification and honor, not in lustful passion, like the Gentiles who do not know God.*"[13]

Paul also promises that we can be victorious over sin. "*No temptation has overtaken you but such as is common to man; and God is faithful, who will not allow you to be tempted beyond what you are able, but with the temptation will provide the way of escape also, so that you will be able to endure it.*"[14] Born-again adults can have victory over sin if they depend upon God's grace in their lives.

Of greater concern was the discovery that so many who were involved in sin did not feel guilty about it. The book, *Cultural Captives*, puts it this way:

> *Over half of those who participated in homosexual thoughts or behavior, living together with a sex partner, or adultery claimed that they had no problem with the*

activity. In other words, even though the Bible clearly states that this behavior is harmful to their life and testimony, they say it is fine for them.[15]

A percentage of these born-again adults admitted to being deceitful. This included a number who struggled with being dishonest and by telling lies (15%). They also had trouble dealing with greed and getting drunk.

Proverbs tell us that the Lord hates a lying tongue.[16] Instead, the Bible commands us to tell the truth. Truth can guide us and lead us to God (Psalm 43:3). God will even lead us in truth (Psalm 25:5). Jesus tells us that the truth will set us free (John 8:31).

The survey demonstrated two issues of concern. Many more in this generation struggle with various unbiblical behaviors than we might expect. But an even greater concern is the fact that many don't actually struggle with the behavior because they don't feel guilty about something the Bible specifically addresses. A few areas in which relatively higher proportions of born-again adults involved in these behaviors did not believe it was wrong included: homosexuality or same-sex attraction, anxiety, and drunkenness.

The relatively high percentage of born-again adults who did not believe anything was wrong with homosexuality or same-sex attraction most likely illustrates the pervasive influence and promotion of the homosexual lifestyle in news, entertainment, and popular culture. Although the Bible labels homosexual behavior as sinful,[17] the cultural messages apparently overwhelm this biblical perspective. In the next chapter we talk about how these cultural influences have made such an impact.

Many involved in sin did not feel any remorse.

Chapter Twenty-Four: Sexuality

1 Thessalonians 4:3 *For this is the will of God, your sanctification; that is, that you abstain from sexual immorality;*

An important aspect of what Christians should believe is a biblical view of sex. In our sex-saturated society, there are all sorts of unbiblical messages about sexuality, and so it is important that a Christian think about sex from a proper perspective and act accordingly.

Some Christian speakers often begin a talk on sex by saying that nothing in the Bible says sex is wrong. The statement is not only meant to shock but to teach an important point. The Bible does not teach that sex is wrong, but it does teach that the improper use of sex is wrong and harmful.

The Bible teaches that sexual purity is a precious treasure that should be valued and even protected. Sexual purity is also becoming a rare commodity in a world that no longer follows biblical principles. We glorify God in our sexuality when we use self-control in the power of the Holy Spirit and stay pure.

God intended that sex be completely contained within marriage. He condemns sex outside of marriage. The Bible uses the word "fornication" or the words "sexual immorality" when speaking about sex outside of marriage. The Greek word is "porneia" and is used forty-four times in the New Testament and includes such things as premarital sex, extramarital sex, and homosexuality. It could even include viewing sexually suggestive material including pornography.

Paul in writing to the Thessalonians said: *"For this is the will of God, your sanctification; that is, that you abstain from sexual immorality; that each of you know how to possess his own vessel in sanctification and honor, not in lustful passion, like the Gentiles who do not know God."*[18]

Paul provides two principles. First, believers are to abstain from sexual immorality. The word "abstain" means to keep away as far as possible. You should stay away from the dangers of sexual promiscuity. Contrary to what many believe, multiple surveys show that living together before marriage results in a higher probability of ending in divorce. Abstinence before marriage is the only way to avoid the physical, emotional, and spiritual problems associated with premarital sex.

Second, Paul teaches that you should control your own body. We should exercise self-control (a topic we will address in more detail in the next chapter). Paul commands us to live in *"sanctification and honor, not in lustful passion, like the Gentiles who do not know God."*

Abstinence results in a higher chance of entering into a successful marriage.

Paul writing to the church in Corinth admonished them to: *"Flee immorality. Every other sin that a man commits is outside the body, but the immoral man sins against his own body. Or do you not know that your body is a temple of the Holy Spirit who is in you, whom you have from God, and that you are not your own? For you have been bought with a price: therefore glorify God in your body."*[19]

With the warning, Paul sets forth some important principles. First, our body is the temple of the Holy Spirit. What we do with our bodies sexually has implications not only to us in the physical realm, but also has spiritual consequences. It certainly means that our bodies do not belong to us. Second, we have been bought with a price (Christ's death on the cross for our sins). That means that our body has been purchased by God. Therefore, we should glorify God in our body.

In his letter to the Galatians, before Paul describes the fruit of the spirit, he provides a list of the deeds of the flesh. *"Now the deeds of the flesh are evident, which are: immorality, impurity, sensuality, idolatry, sorcery, enmities, strife, jealousy, outbursts of anger, disputes, dissensions, factions, envying, drunkenness, carousing, and things like these, of which I forewarn you, just as I have forewarned you, that those who practice such things will not inherit the kingdom of God."*[20]

How are Christians acting concerning their sexual behavior? Probe Ministries' study of born-again, young adults paints a disturbing picture of Christian sexuality.[95] The respondents reported having difficulties or challenges with various sexual issues (e.g. sex prior to marriage, watching pornography, etc.). The survey also found that those without a biblical worldview were more than twice as likely to deny that sexual issues are a problem. Put another way, those with a biblical worldview may struggle with sexual issues but usually feel guilt about their struggles. Those without a biblical worldview are much more likely not to feel any guilt or see their actions as a problem.

We should feel guilty when we violate God's laws and principles concerning sexuality. But the good news is that if we confess our sin and put our trust in Christ, He will forgive us and give us a holy lifestyle. The Bible promises, *"If we confess our sins, he is faithful and just and will forgive us our sins and purify us from all unrighteousness."*[21] God is ready to forgive us, cleanse us, and purify us from our sins.

Those without a biblical worldview were more than twice as likely to deny that sexual immorality is a sin.

Chapter 25: Flee Immorality

1 Corinthians 6:19-20 *Your body is a temple of the Holy Spirit within you, whom you have from God? You are not your own, for you were bought with a price. So glorify God in your body*

There is an important principle running through this section. The principle is that "the world and the flesh are enticing us to live in ways that negate our testimony." We should live differently from the world in many ways, and one of the ways we should be different is how we deal with immorality.

In the previous chapter we talked about the fact that sexual purity is a precious treasure and often a rare commodity in culture. Christians, captivated by the culture, live and dress like the rest of the culture. As Christians we are called "out of darkness" into light because we are now "the people of God."[22]

Our analysis of multiple surveys of born-again, emerging adults found that fewer than one in five expressed a biblical worldview understanding on sexual issues; e.g. sex before marriage, casual sex, pornography. The Probe Survey indicates that over 60% of them have participated in sexually related activities outside of marriage.

We have already discussed the biblical concept found in Paul's admonition to the church in Corinth. He said that we are to: "flee immorality."[23] Later in his letter, he calls upon Christians to: "flee from idolatry."[24] In another letter, Paul instructs Timothy and the church to: "flee from youthful lusts."[25] It should be pretty obvious then that Paul is sharing an important principle. When sins like immorality and idolatry could affect our lives and our testimony, we are to run away.

We live in a world of temptation (addressed in more detail in a later chapter). This was true in Paul's day, and it is true today. In fact, because of the influence of the media and its pervasive influence, we may be facing even more powerful and invasive temptations in the twenty-first century than in the first century.

Unfortunately, we often don't talk about lust and sexual temptation within the church or even among ourselves. We may be too proud to admit that we are tempted. We may be embarrassed that we struggle with such temptations. Our society has lowered its standards so much that we don't even realize the depth of our temptation and sin. And we may avoid the conversation because we enjoy looking at sensual movies and television programs and visiting various Internet websites.

As Christians living in a sex-saturated society, we need to take specific steps to protect ourselves from the influence of the culture. Otherwise we will become culturally captive Christians whose testimony brings reproach upon the gospel.

First, we should remove sexually explicit and sexually immoral media and material from our lives. The Proverbs warn us to "guard our heart" because it is the "wellspring of life."[26] Job talks about making a "covenant with my eyes" so he would not look lustfully at another woman.[27] Isaiah instructs us to shut our "eyes from looking upon evil."[28] Paul admonishes Christians to "rid yourselves of all such things as these: anger, rage, malice, slander, and filthy language from your lips."[29]

Second, we should replace it with positive influences. Paul says that we are to think on the things which are true, noble, right, pure, lovely, admirable, excellent, and praiseworthy.[30] We should commit ourselves to a daily reading of the Bible. We should commit ourselves to a pattern of daily prayer.

Hold one another accountable in this area of sexual purity.

Third, we should also have other Christians in our lives. They can pray for us and keep us accountable. And they can prevent us from being led astray by the sin of the world around us. Proverbs warns us that "if sinners entice you, do not consent."[31] It also warns us not to "walk in the way with them [sinners], keep your feet from their path."[32]

Finally, we should also develop discernment so that we can recognize danger areas of temptation and flee from such situations and circumstances. Certainly this comes with spiritual maturity but it also comes from reading God's word and applying it to our daily lives.

God wants us to live a holy life. Peter reminds us that we are to be "like the Holy One who called you, be holy yourselves also in all your behavior; because it is written, you shall be holy, for I am holy."[33] When we live a holy life, we provide a positive testimony of Christ to the world.

Make the effort to develop a discerning spirit to help you avoid the sexual temptations of our culture.

Chapter 26: Appetites and Passions

Colossians 3:1-3 *Therefore if you have been raised up with Christ, keep seeking the things above, where Christ is, seated at the right hand of God. Set your mind on the things above, not on the things that are on earth.*

In the verse above, Paul reminds us who we are and what we should seek – the things above, where Christ is. Even as Christians, we struggle with certain attitudes and behaviors. It is comforting to know that the Apostle Paul also struggled with the reality that sometimes we do what we should not do. He admitted this in his letter to the church in Rome. "*For what I am doing, I do not understand; for I am not practicing what I would like to do, but I am doing the very thing I hate. . . . For the good that I want, I do not do, but I practice the very evil that I do not want.*"[34]

Paul explained that Christians are no longer under obligation to the Old Testament ceremonial law. But that doesn't mean that we should feel free to act as we would like. If we are to carry out our eternal purpose, we must walk closely with God in obedience. Paul exhorts us to set our hearts on heaven seeking the things which are above and not the things of earth. One reason we should do this, he says, is because Christ sits at the right hand of God. He has gone before us to heaven, and we should seek to follow Him in what we do here on earth.

Some translations say we should set "our affections" on the things above. Our mind and emotions should be set on the things above not on the things of the earth. It is easy to understand why this is a challenge for us. We were born into this world and are interested and involved in things pertaining to earthly life. It is easy to get wrapped up in those things. But we shouldn't be too comfortable in this world since we are merely travelers passing through this place. A. W. Tozer said, "Pilgrims have not yet found that place they can call home"[35]

In the following verses, Paul lists the appetites and passions that we are to put aside. Some translations say we are to "mortify" these things; i.e. put them to death. "*Therefore consider the members of your earthly body as dead to immorality, impurity, passion, evil desire, and greed, which amounts to idolatry. For it is because of these things that the wrath of God will come upon the sons of disobedience, and in them you also once walked, when you were living in them.*"[36]

We are to consider our bodies dead to the lusts of the flesh. This would include sexual immorality, impurity, passion (inordinate affection), and evil desire. These were activities that they indulged in their former live but are contrary to the Christian life. He also lists greed which he calls idolatry. In essence, Paul is warning us not to love the world so much that we make an idol of it. He goes on to explain that we once walked in this way, but we are not to do so as believers.

Don't make worldly pleasures an idol.

Not only are we to put aside (mortify) our appetites, but Paul tells us to put aside inordinate passions. "*But now you also, put them all aside: anger, wrath, malice, slander, and abusive speech from your mouth.*"[37] Adding in the next verse, we are not to lie to one another. These behaviors are contrary to the life God created us to live. Anger is bad, but malice can even be worse because it is premeditated. Slander and abusive speech (also translated filthy communication) are expressions of the heart that are a product of the tongue. And lying is contrary to the law of truth and the law of love.

Are these inappropriate actions problems for Christians today? In Probe Ministry's study of born-again, young adults, we discovered they did indeed struggle with these behaviors.[95] Nearly half of them admitted they were challenged by anger (47%) and by impatience (47%). Almost as many express that they struggle with cursing (45%). Over one-third of these adults grapple with losing their temper (36%) or gossiping (35%). It is worth noting that for born-again, young adults with a biblical worldview, their biggest struggles were with anger and impatience. For those without a biblical worldview, their biggest struggle was with cursing and swearing.

Well over half (~60%) of them admit to some type of sexual sin, sex outside of marriage, adultery, homosexuality, or pornography. Even those young adults with a biblical worldview had almost 50% admit to sexual sin. Almost one third of those without a biblical worldview who engaged in these behaviors admitted they did not feel guilty about them.

The study also found that these born-again adults are struggling with deceitful behavior. This included struggling with "being dishonest" and "challenged by telling lies." They also admitted trying to deal with greed.

Overall, looking across 25 sinful activities, a majority believe that one or more of these behaviors are wrong, but engage in them anyway. Many of those who engage do not feel guilt about their actions. Obviously, we need to focus on the instructions in Colossians. We are to put to death these appetites and set aside these behaviors. We are called to set our minds and affections on the things above and live lives of holiness that glorify God.

One of the songs in the *Now I'm Bound* CD is "In This House."[17] The lyrics remind us that we should not let our life be about anger, selfish gain, or worldly things.

In this house, no more anger
In this house, no more selfish gain
In this house, hope and love will remain
You've taught us well to return to the Lord, our Savior

Acknowledge activities God warns us against and rely on His Spirit to help us avoid them.

Chapter 27: Put on a New Man

Col. 3:10 *Put on the new self who is being renewed to a true knowledge according to the image of the One who created him.*

We all know that it is important to dress the part. If you are going to play baseball or basketball or football, you need to dress appropriately. If you are in the military, you need to wear a uniform. In law enforcement, you need to wear a uniform and a badge. In the old book, *Dress for Success*, the author provided readers who wanted to climb the corporate ladder with a relatively simple advice: dress like your boss.

In his letter to the Colossians, Paul describes how Christians are to dress. He isn't talking about the clothes we wear. He isn't saying we should wear a T-shirt that says "Jesus Saves" or "I Am Second." Certainly there is nothing wrong with letting people know you are a Christian. But he is focusing on the need for us as Christians to put on a new man. "*Do not lie to one another, since you laid aside the old self with its evil practices, and have put on the new self who is being renewed to a true knowledge according to the image of the One who created him-a renewal in which there is no distinction between Greek and Jew, circumcised and uncircumcised, barbarian, Scythian, slave and freeman, but Christ is all, and in all.*"[38]

If you are a Christian, you should dress the part. A new man should wear new clothes. As a Christian, you should "look the part." As noted in the last chapter, Paul reminded the believers that they should set their minds and affections on the things above. The internal change in their lives should have an outward manifestation. Our lifestyle should not be captive to the culture but should reflect the truth of the gospel.

C.S. Lewis reminds us that the "Christian way is different: harder, and easier. Christ says, 'Give me All. I don't want so much of your time and so much of your money and so much of your work: I want You." He therefore concludes that "the almost impossible thing, is to hand over your whole self—all your wishes and precautions—to Christ. But it is far easier than what we are all trying to do instead."[39]

Paul asks us to do two things. First, get rid of the old as discussed in the last chapter. Second, we are to put on the new man. In order to be effective, we need to distinguish between the old man and the new man.

The Bible teaches that the old man and our old life was crucified. "For if we have become united with Him in the likeness of His death, certainly we shall also be in the likeness of His resurrection, knowing this, that our old self was crucified with Him, in order that our body of sin might be done away with, so that we would no longer be slaves to sin."[40] In another passage, Paul says, *"I have been crucified with Christ; and it is no longer I who live, but Christ lives in me; and the life which I now live in the flesh I live by faith in the Son of God, who loved me and gave Himself up for me."*[41]

Your old way of living has been crucified with Christ.

Not only was the old man crucified, but it was also corrupt. Paul instructs believers "to put off your old self, which belongs to your former manner of life and is corrupt through deceitful desires."[42] It was our sin nature subject to temptation and sin (a topic we address in more detail in subsequent chapters).

What is the new man? It has always been God's plan though marred by the Fall. He gives us a new nature, not just a revised old man but a new man. Because of this, we can live and should live differently than the way the nonbelievers live in the world. There are a number of characteristics of the new man:

1. Christians are to walk differently: *"So this I say, and affirm together with the Lord, that you walk no longer just as the Gentiles also walk, in the futility of their mind"*[43]

Christians are to be different from the world in the way they walk and conduct their lives.

2. Christians are to walk in love. *"Therefore be imitators of God, as beloved children; and walk in love, just as Christ also loved you and gave Himself up for us, an offering and a sacrifice to God as a fragrant aroma."*[44] We are to express love just as we have received God's love

3. Christians are to walk with wisdom. *"Therefore be careful how you walk, not as unwise men but as wise, making the most of your time, because the days are evil."*[45] We are to walk in wisdom and discernment unlike the unbelievers around us.

Finally, we should understand how this takes place. Paul says that the new man is renewed to a true knowledge according to the image of God. Later, we will explore how to renew our minds. For now, let's look at one passage connecting the idea of a new man to the concept of being renewed in our minds. In Ephesians, Paul commanded them to *"lay aside the old self, which is being corrupted in accordance with the lusts of deceit, and that you be renewed in the spirit of your mind, and put on the new self, which in the likeness of God has been created in righteousness and holiness of the truth."*[46]

As a Christian with a new nature, you should be continually renewed by the true knowledge of the image of God. While it is true that the image of God in us was affected by the Fall, we should also recognize that we can be renewed day by day.[47] We are being renewed by the Holy Spirit so that we will be *"conformed to the image of Christ."*[48] And the Holy Spirit is also renewing the spirit of the mind.[49] As we walk in Christ and grow in grace, we are becoming more like Christ.

We are to walk in Christ, bearing His image.

Chapter 28: Love and Fear

1 John 4:18-19 *There is no fear in love, but perfect love casts out fear, because fear involved punishment, and the one who fears is not perfected in love. We love, because He first loved us.*

Going through this study, you probably have experienced a range of emotions (surprise, disbelief, guilt). Fortunately God provides perspective on how you should react emotionally to this study, "*perfect love casts out fear*".[50] The Bible teaches in some instances fear can be helpful to our Christian walk and in others it can be quite harmful. Fear of God is good. But groundless, irrational fear produces anxiety rather than peace.

We are to have a healthy fear of God. Proverbs teaches that fear of God is important in gaining wisdom: "*The fear of the LORD is the beginning of wisdom.*"[51] It also teaches that fear is an antidote to pride and arrogance: "*Do not be wise in your own eyes; Fear the LORD and turn away from evil.*"[52] It also teaches the physical benefits of fearing the Lord: "*The fear of the LORD leads to life, So that one may sleep satisfied, untouched by evil.*"[53]

The Bible also teaches us NOT to fear. Joshua told his men not to fear, but be strong and courageous.[54] Elijah told the widow not to fear.[55] God told Isaiah not to fear: "*For I am the Lord your God, who upholds your right hand, Who says to you, ' Do not fear, I will help you.*"[56] God also told Jeremiah[57] and Daniel[58] not to fear.

Jesus taught His disciples not to fear. "*Do not fear those who kill the body but are unable to kill the soul; but rather fear Him who is able to destroy both soul and body in hell. . . .So do not fear; you are more valuable than many sparrows.*"[59] The apostle Paul reminds us: "*God has not given us the spirit of fear; but of power, and of love, and of a sound mind.*"[60] We are not to live in a spirit of fear, but with the double blessing of power and love.

Why do we fear? Often it is because we feel powerless over our circumstances. We may not know where our next paycheck

 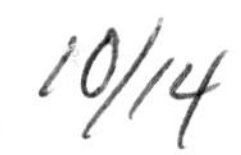

is coming from or what the doctor is going to tell us about our health. We fret that we cannot change our circumstances. When we feel helpless and powerless, fear is often the first emotion we feel. We can literally become worried sick over our status or things from our past. Fear makes our lives miserable.

Fear causes us to over-compensate. If you have been abused, you may no longer trust people and refuse to be vulnerable. You may be a perfectionist having a feeling that you never measure up. A workaholic may be trying to do more than God expects.

Fear can make us ineffective. You may not work at relationships because you fear rejection. You may never share your faith fearing what others may think. You avoid serving in the church, because you fear you will not do a good job. That is not what God wants. Jesus asked His disciples, *"Why are you afraid, you men of little faith?"*[61] Perfect love casts out fear. We do not have to fear that God loves us or we have not measured up to God's standards for our lives. But we live a life of obedience to Him out of gratitude.

Do not fear. God loves you.

This promise is a favorite among Christians, but sometimes misunderstood. Many of us get stuck on that word "perfect." None of us live perfect lives leading to an important question: Does this promise only apply to perfect people? The word "perfect" comes from the Greek word "telos" meaning goal. A more accurate translation would be: "that stage which has been able to achieve its goal." This fits with other passages where John proclaims that *"whoever keeps His word, in him the love of God has truly been perfected."*[62] He also says that *"if we love one another, God abides in us, and His love is perfected in us."*[63]

We are going to feel fear, guilt, and even regret. But God does not want us to stay in that emotional state of affairs. He poured out his unconditional love to us through his Holy Spirit,[64] so that we would live godly lives. The problem is that often we are afraid to surrender to God's love because of hurts in our past.

We suddenly confront the "what if" questions. What if I surrender to this love and am hurt like in childhood? What if I surrender to this love and still feel abandoned? What if I reveal myself and am rejected? The answer to all of these questions is God's love is perfect. We may not live perfect lives. But God is the epitome of perfection. God's love for us is unconditional and perfect. This love is what we call grace.

Philip Yancey tells of a conference where experts debated what if any belief was unique to the Christian faith. They eliminated various possibilities. The incarnation? No, other religions told of gods appearing as humans. The resurrection? Other religions have people returning from the dead. As the debate unfolded, C.S. Lewis wandered in asking, "What's the rumpus about?" When told, Lewis responded, "Oh, that's easy. It's grace." After some discussion, the conferees had to agree. Yancey concludes: "The Buddhist eight-fold path, the Hindu doctrine of karma, the Jewish covenant, and the Muslim code of law—each of these offers a way to earn approval. Only Christianity dares to make God's love unconditional."[65]

The God of the Bible is unlike the gods of other religions. Only the true God forgives our offense and teaches us to forgive. Only God provides us with the spiritual resources to be obedient to His command. Only God provided a way for salvation by sending His Son to be sin on our behalf.

Yes, it is true that we are guilty before God because of our sin. That is why we feel guilty. We try to do good works, but that is not enough to earn salvation. The good news is that we have been saved through God's grace. Paul explains that *"if you confess with your mouth Jesus as Lord, and believe in your heart that God raised Him from the dead, you will be saved."*[66] God's grace is the best news humanity has ever received.

God's grace overcomes all fear.

Chapter 29: Our Walk, Weapons, and Warfare

2nd Cor. 10:3-5 *For though we walk in the flesh, we do not war according to the flesh, for the weapons of our warfare are not of the flesh, but divinely powerful for the destruction of fortresses. We are destroying speculations and every lofty thing raised up against the knowledge of God, and we are taking every thought captive to the obedience of Christ.*

Paul spoke to an important aspect of Christian living in the preceding passage. When we view the world from an eternal perspective, we are able to destroy those thoughts that take us captive and keep us from living a life pleasing to Him. We begin to understand that the world is not our home, but we are just passing through. We are also aware that the world, the flesh, and the Devil oppose biblical thinking and living. And we are motivated to demolish ideas that are opposed to God's Truth.

In the passage above, Paul talks about three things: our walk, our weapons, and our warfare.

Our walk: He begins by reminding us that "though we walk in the flesh, we do not war according to the flesh." Our battle on this earth is not an earthly one but a spiritual one. So even though we do walk in the flesh, our warfare is not fleshly.

This is one of the reasons it is so easy to become culturally captive. We live in the world and thus are influenced by worldly temptations. We live in the flesh and are tempted by the flesh. Jesus commands us to live godly lives in the world. As Christians we are called to live in this world but not be of this world.[1]

As we have discussed in previous chapters, many Christians have become casualties in this spiritual war. This war against us started long before we came on the scene. And if we are to be successful, we must be willing to fight. Many wars in the past have been lost because people have refused to fight. This is also true of the spiritual war around us today.

The failure of Christians to be victorious over sin and to live the Christian life is actually due to two factors. The first we have already stated: Christians have often been unwilling to fight and have merely gone along with the culture. The second reason for Christian compromise is that so many Christians have not even been aware that there is a spiritual battle.

To be successful, we must do a number of things. We must separate ourselves from the influence of the world, and we must stand and fight the evil that threatens our lives, our families, our communities, our nation, and our world.

<u>Our weapons:</u> Paul teaches that *"the weapons of our warfare are not of the flesh, but divinely powerful for the destruction of fortresses."* One of the most important weapons of our warfare is the Word of God. Paul calls it the "Sword of the Spirit."[2] Psalm 119 says the Bible helps cleanse the spirit so that a believer will not sin against the Lord.[3] The Bible is a weapon in our hands that we can take to the uttermost parts of the earth.[4]

We are instructed to wear armor before we go into battle.[5] We are to gird our loins with truth; defining the truth, defending the truth, and spreading the truth. We are also to wear the breastplate of righteousness relying on the righteousness of Jesus to live holy lives. We are also to take up the shield of faith. When we have bold faith, we are able to extinguish all of Satan's attacks. And we are to take the helmet of salvation. We need to be assured of our salvation and stand firm in that assurance. We need to think and act consistently with our position in Christ.

Our spiritual weapons are divinely powerful

<u>Our warfare:</u> What is the goal of our conflict with the world? Paul says: *"We are destroying speculations and every lofty thing raised up against the knowledge of God, and we are taking every thought captive to the obedience of Christ."*

First, we are to destroy something. The word "speculations" (sometimes translated "imaginations") refers to the mind. This would include our thoughts and our reflections. We are to challenge the false ideas that Satan has encouraged in the world by countering unbiblical speculations and proclaiming God's truth. As we noted in previous chapters, often these ideas are taught and promoted by false teachers.

Second, we are to take every thought captive. Throughout this book we have quoted Colossians saying *"see to it that no one takes you captive through philosophy and empty deception."*[6] The same word "captive" appears in both verses. Essentially, as believers, we should take every thought captive otherwise we will be taken captive by the false ideas of the world.

Paul calls for us to walk in this world but not be worldly. He admonishes us to pull down the strongholds of Satan in this world. He calls for us to take every thought captive so that we will not be taken captive by the false philosophies of the world.

As we walk in Christ, the lyrics of one of the songs in the CD that accompanies this teaching program could even be our prayer.[17] The song "Love Like This" challenges us to walk this earth with wisdom.

Make me wise to walk this earth, And gentle like You, Father.
Joyful like child, secure. Make me brave to speak Your words
Give faith that beckons miracles make me pure and wholly Yours.

I want to be like You. I only want to be found faithful
Lord make us able to represent You well.
Give me eyes to read the hearts of men, inspire hope to risk again
And take chances for your Kingdom
I choose today to spend my life for them.

Watch your thoughts; align them with Christ.

Chapter 30: Taking Thoughts Captive

2nd Cor. 10:5 *We are destroying speculations and every lofty thing raised up against the knowledge of God, and we are taking every thought captive to the obedience of Christ.*

Proper biblical thinking is a precursor to biblical living. We cannot live in a way that pleases God unless we are able to think biblically about life. We must take every thought captive in obedience to Christ. What does that mean, and how do we do it?

Let's return to the key verse listed above. Earlier in this passage, and in his letter to the Ephesians,[7] Paul makes it clear that we are not fighting against people but rather against speculations. The word "speculations" has also been translated as fortresses or strongholds. A word taken from the military, it is used only once in the Bible. It describes a castle with walls, towers, and moats. It is strongly defended by soldiers who plan to hold out for weeks and months against any attack.

In this context, fortresses are the false ideas that promote evil and error. Paul continues by saying that we are destroying "speculations raised up against the knowledge of Christ." Those who are taken captive by wrong thoughts[8] are to be released by the truth of the Bible so that they can take every thought captive to the obedience of Christ.

Our thoughts come from three sources: God, the Devil, and ourselves. If we are thinking biblically, then our thoughts parallel God's thoughts. Astronomer Johann Kepler said he was "thinking God's thoughts after Him." That is a good way to explain how we are to think biblical thoughts. However, the contrary is also true. If we are thinking like the world then our thoughts most likely parallel Satan's thoughts.

How do we recognize whether we are thinking God's thoughts or the Devil's? One way is to compare your thoughts to the principles in God's Word. Paul told the Philippians to let their minds "dwell on these things."

> *Finally, brethren, whatever is true, whatever is honorable, whatever is right, whatever is pure, whatever is lovely, whatever is of good repute, if there is any excellence and if anything worthy of praise, dwell on these things.*[9]

What is the opposite of truth? Lies, falsehood, dishonesty, and deception would be the opposite of truth. What is the opposite of honorable? Dishonorable, deceptive, manipulative, and gossip would be the opposite of honorable. Unclean, sinful, filthy, and degrading would be the opposite of pure. Do your thoughts line up with biblical truth?

Our goal: Have the mind of Christ

Any thoughts that we have that do not correspond with Scripture, are probably not from God. They may be our thoughts or Satan's thoughts. They may be false ideas planted in our minds. They may be temptations from the world, the flesh, or the Devil. Our goal should be to have "the mind of Christ" so that we are not thinking any negative or unbiblical thoughts.[10]

As believers we need to activate the "mind of Christ" that is already in us but must become first in our thinking. We need to know God's thoughts, and we understand His thoughts by reading God's Word. Then we should evaluate those thoughts. Proverbs says that God "weighs the spirits"[11] and we are to do the same. This involves spiritual discernment which will provide us with a biblical grid to determine truth from error.

We are also commanded to throw out the thoughts that are not of God. This is one way we can tear down strongholds. Is this thought from God? If not, does it contradict Scripture? These are important questions we should ask all the time if we want to develop the "mind of Christ."

While it is tempting to blame Satan for the sinful thoughts in our minds, we should acknowledge that often sinful thoughts come from our sinful nature. Jesus taught that what comes from us is often what defiles us.

> *That which proceeds out of the man, that is what defiles the man. For from within, out of the heart of men, proceed the evil thoughts, fornications, thefts, murders, adulteries, deeds of coveting and wickedness, as well as deceit, sensuality, envy, slander, pride and foolishness. All these evil things proceed from within and defile the man.*[12]

This should not be a surprise since the Bible clearly teaches that the "heart is more deceitful than all else."[13] On the other hand, we must also understand that merely having such thoughts is not necessarily sin. As we will discuss more later, James explains that sin comes when we dwell on these thoughts and act upon them.[14]

When Paul wrote to the Christians in Rome he wanted them to conform to the image of Christ.[15] But he also expressed his concern that they might be conformed to the world. "*And do not be conformed to this world, but be transformed by the renewing of your mind, so that you may prove what the will of God is, that which is good and acceptable and perfect.*"[16]

If we are taking captive every thought, we won't be captive to the world's philosophies. And if we are conformed to the image of Christ, we won't be conformed to this world. The key is to make sure that every day we are being transformed by the renewing of our minds. His mercies are new each morning.[17] Start each day with Him and with His Word. This is an important step in thinking and living biblically.

Let Christ actively renew your mind.

Chapter 31: Life is a Test

1st Peter 1:7 *Such trials show the proven character of your faith, which is much more valuable than gold—gold that is tested by fire, even though it is passing away—and will bring praise and glory and honor when Jesus Christ is revealed.*

You have probably wondered about the concept that life is a test. Likely, you hated taking tests in school and don't welcome the idea that living in this world is a test. The Bible says testing often comes in the form of trials and temptations. In fact, these words (trials, testing, temptation, etc.) appear more than 200 times in the Bible. Yes, life is a test.

It is not enough to have right thinking. We need right motivations and right actions. Testing is one way to reveal and develop proper motivations and actions. In the Monopoly board game there is a card known as the "Get Out of Jail" card. Many of us would like to have a "Get Out of Trials and Suffering" card. But life does not work that way. We cannot expect to be exempt from testing when the people in the Bible went through testing.

In Genesis, we see God testing Abraham's faith. Although the reason may be shrouded in mystery, the test was obvious. God asked Abraham to sacrifice his son Isaac. Abraham knew the character of God. He could count on Him to be good and faithful. Yet, God tested and thereby strengthened Abraham's faith.

Joseph eventually served as prime minister over all of Egypt. But the trip he took to that distinguished post included slavery and humiliation long before exaltation. He found that often the way up is a road that takes you down.

God allowed Job to be tested by Satan. He allowed Satan and the world to see that Job's faithfulness was not because of any physical comfort. Job's suffering was not due to some fault in him, for God makes it clear both in the beginning and ending of the book that Job is unlike any other in his righteousness.

David was ultimately destined to be king over Israel. But he started as a shepherd boy. Before he ruled as king he served in King Saul's household and learned important lessons about jealousy and the corrupting influence of power. Many times he barely escaped with his life as Saul sought to kill him. Though he eventually ruled as Israel's king, he faced many trials and tests.

It is also worth noting that not all of the biblical characters passed their tests. David certainly did not. Sampson did not. Even Adam and Eve failed their test in the Garden of Eden. Many passed their tests successfully, like Joseph and Daniel, Ruth and Esther. Others were not successful.

Trials strengthen our character

Why does God allow us to be tested? Trials and tests reveal, strengthen, and develop our character. David asked God to test him and examine his heart and mind to see that they were true to Him.[18] In reality we are always being tested. God is watching our response to the problems, obstacles, and frustrations we face each day. In the testing, we can see if our faith is real and making a difference in our lives and the lives of those around us.

Jesus tells a parable using what happens when the sower's seed hits different types of soil.[19] Some receive God's Word with joy, but soon fall away as a time of testing comes. As shallow Christians, their faith withers when the hot sun of persecution comes. They are too weak to endure the testing.

James explains that testing of our faith produces perseverance, which results in spiritual maturity.[20] James also says that testing is a blessing because when it is finished, we will have stood the test and will receive *"the crown of life which the Lord has promised to those who love Him."*[21] Trials and testing come from God who works all things together for good for those who love Him and are called to be the children of God.[22]

Testing in the Bible is often compared to the refining of precious metal. In the Psalms, for example, our testing is likened to being refined like silver.[23] In our introductory verse, Peter says that the trials in our lives are similar to gold being refined to remove all of its impurities.[24] Do you have impurities in your life? Testing can remove them.

It is hard to predict God's tests, but we get some clues from Scripture. God certainly will test your heart. In Proverbs it says *"fire tests the purity of silver and gold, but the Lord tests the heart."*[25] David called on God to test his motives and heart.[26] God will also test your response to changes, problems, obstacles, and tragedies. You may be the target of persecution. You may face undeserved criticism or suffer because of malicious gossip.

God may also withdraw from you. Many of us (including people in the Bible) have struggled with the silence of God. How will you react when you can no longer feel the presence of God? The Bible records the story of the Old Testament king Hezekiah. It says that *"God left him alone only to test him, that He might know all that was in his heart."*[27] God might leave you alone as an important test of our faith.

Realizing that life is a test, you begin to see everything you think, say, and do as significant. You are not only being tested in how you face adversity. You are also being tested in how you treat a clerk in a store or a waitress in a restaurant. Are you demonstrating the love of Christ in those actions as well?

When testing comes our way, receive it with joy because God will use it to strengthen our faith. When we are knocked down, we are dependent upon Him. We should *"consider it all joy"* when we *"encounter various trials, knowing that the testing of your faith produces endurance."*[28] Yes, life is a test.

Receive testing with joy.
God will use it to strengthen you.

Chapter 32: Trials

James 1:2 *Consider it all joy, my brethren, when you encounter various trials, knowing that the testing of your faith produces endurance.*

Life is hard. We will face trials whether we are young or old, rich or poor, healthy or sick. Some of us might face fewer trials than others, but all of us face trials. As in the last chapter, life is a test. There will be testing of your faith. And God will use the trials and circumstances of your life to build character in you.

People often talk about the promises of Jesus. Many of those promises are positive, wonderful and encouraging. For example, Jesus said that He came that we might have life *"and have it abundantly."*[29] While we may bask in the promise of an abundant life, we must remember that Jesus promised in this world we would have tribulation. But He also comforts us with the promise that He has "overcome the world."[30]

All people face trials. Yet Jesus is saying that because we are Christians, we will also face trials and tribulations in the world. We won't be insulated from pain, suffering, and the daily trials of life. In fact, Peter actually teaches that trials are a normal part of life. Writing to Christians facing trials and persecution, he said: *"Beloved, do not be surprised at the fiery ordeal among you, which comes upon you for your testing, as though some strange thing were happening to you."*[31] We should not see trials as strange or unusual. They are part of the Christian life.

How are we to respond to trials in our lives? James says we are to: *"Consider it all joy, my brethren, when you encounter various trials, knowing that the testing of your faith produces endurance. And let endurance have its perfect result, so that you may be perfect and complete, lacking in nothing."*[32]

First, we are to express joy in the midst of trials. We see this in the lives of the apostles in the first century. The book of Acts recounts many times when they expressed joy in the midst of trials and persecution.[33] They could express joy because they could see through the trials. The writer of Hebrews says that we are to *"run with endurance the race that is set before us, fixing our eyes on Jesus, the author and perfecter of faith, who for the joy set before Him endured the cross, despising the shame, and has sat down at the right hand of the throne of God."*[34] And Peter reminds us that we are being *"tested by fire."*[35]

Second, we are to know that the testing of our faith produces endurance and patience. Just as a runner can increase his or her endurance by running longer and further each day, so we can increase our endurance through the trials we face. Someone who wants to run a marathon doesn't accomplish the task by just going out and running the race. The runner uses varying trials of distance and pace in order to be able to run the race with endurance.

Trials produce patience and endurance.

Third, these trials are to produce in you "a perfect result." Trials produce patience and endurance. Patience and endurance produce spiritual maturity. They will make you perfect and complete so that you lack nothing. Peter explains that a spiritually mature Christian has learned to lean totally upon Christ for strength.[36]

We do not expect a baby to remain a baby. We expect the baby to grow and mature into a child and eventually into a mature adult. Likewise, God does not expect you to remain a spiritual baby.[37] He wants to use the circumstances of your life so that you become spiritually mature.

Another key passage that relates to trials is Paul's declaration to the church in Rome. He explains: *"And we know that God causes all things to work together for good to those who love God, to those who are called according to His purpose."*[38] This verse may unfortunately be the most misused and misunderstood passage in the Bible. It doesn't mean that God causes all trials and evil. It doesn't mean that God will make everything right in this world. It doesn't mean that God will bring a happy ending to all the trials you face on this earth. What does it mean?

First, Paul says "we know." That means we can rest in the assurance that God is in control. We can trust in a sovereign God even if we don't understand what He is doing in our lives or the world right now.

Second, Paul says that "God causes all things to work together." He is behind what is happening in the world, but He is not the cause of evil and suffering in the world. God is using trials in our lives to achieve a greater purpose in our lives. Moreover, the trials and actions are not working independently of each other, but God is working all of them together.

Third, Paul says that God is working them together "for good." That doesn't mean that everything that is happening is good. The opposite is true. Evil, pain, and suffering are in the world because of sin and the Fall. But God is using the actions and circumstances in the world for good in our lives.

Finally, Paul reminds us that this promise is for "those who are called according to His purpose." It is not a promise for all of humankind. It is a promise only for believers. And what is His purpose? Our purpose should be to become more like Christ.

The Bible teaches that we will face trials. We cannot prevent the trials from coming, but we can respond appropriately to them. Paul tells us that *"in everything give thanks; for this is God's will for you in Christ Jesus."*[39] We should give thanks for what God brings in our lives and express joy. This is a great challenge for us, but it is what God is calling for us to do when we encounter trials in our lives.

Express joy in your trials, knowing God is at work.

Chapter 33: Temptations

1st Cor. 10:13b *God . . . will not allow you to be tempted beyond what you are able, but with the temptation will provide the way of escape also, so that you will be able to endure it*

We live in a world filled with temptation. So how do we deal with it? The world's view is that you simply give into it. Perhaps it is a fatalism that was best expressed by Oscar Wilde who once said, "I can resist anything except temptation." As believers we are to resist temptation and not give into it. To be successful, understand how it works in your life. It begins with a desire within us starting with the mind. Jesus said, *"For from within, out of the heart of men, proceed the evil thoughts, fornications, thefts, murders, adulteries, deeds of coveting and wickedness, as well as deceit, sensuality, envy, slander, pride and foolishness. All these evil things proceed from within and defile the man."*[40] The starting point of temptation is within you.

In Corinthians, Paul describes seven important truths about temptation. *"Therefore let him who thinks he stands take heed that he does not fall. No temptation has overtaken you but such as is common to man; and God is faithful, who will not allow you to be tempted beyond what you are able, but with the temptation will provide the way of escape also, so that you will be able to endure it."*[41] Let's look at each of these truths in more detail.

1. Don't think you cannot fall. Thinking you are immune to temptation, puts you in dangerous territory. Many godly people have fallen into sin thinking they could not fall. History is full of believers who thought "it can't happen to me." Sometimes we think temptation is not a problem. We are not tempted to kill or steal. We aren't tempted by drugs and alcohol. So we can erroneously conclude temptation is not a problem. This verse reminds us it is.

2. Temptations can overtake you. A common misconception is that temptations are neutral. We can take them or leave

them. But this passage actually teaches that temptations can grab hold of you and pull you down. Think of a wide receiver that catches the ball and sprints toward the end zone only to be caught and dragged to the ground. That is how temptations grab you and defeat you.

3. Your temptations are not unique. Paul says that these temptations are "common to man." We may rationalize "no one understands the pressure I am under" or "no one feels the temptations I feel." The temptations around you are common to others. You are not unique in feeling them.

4. God is faithful. God will not abandon you. He won't let temptations of the world destroy you. But we must do our part to protect ourselves. Proverbs tells us that we should guard our heart.[42] We can be tempted by the world, the flesh, and the devil. Our outward actions may not be in line with our heart. God warned "*people draw near with their mouth and honor me with their lips, while their hearts are far from me.*"[43] Guard your hearts to be right with God.

5. God only permits what you can withstand. This important principle comforts us when we face temptation. God "*will not allow you to be tempted beyond what you are able.*" implies there are different levels of temptation for people. A group of people walk past a bar. Most wouldn't think about walking in. But some may feel the temptation to go in and get drunk. A group of people walk past a casino. Most wouldn't even think about it. Some might be tempted to gamble. Each person has different experiences and desires. Something that might be a great temptation for one person might not be much of a temptation for another.

6. God provides a way of escape. Not only does temptation come with limits, but there is an escape hatch. Often the way out is to get out. In the next verse, Paul commands us to "flee from idolatry."[44] Earlier, Paul tells us to "flee immorality."[45] So while there is a way of escape in every

situation, often it is to leave the situation. In "The Matrix" Cypher gives Neo a piece of advice: "When you see an agent, you do what we do. Run." This is good advice for the Christian. Many times that way of escape is to flee.

7. God will help you bear it. Paul encourages us by reminding us that God will help us to endure it. We can be successful in dealing with temptation if we trust in Him.

Temptation by itself is not sin. The writer of Hebrews explains that Jesus was "*tempted in all things as we are*" yet he did not sin.[46] Jesus was holy and pure and without sin yet experienced temptation.

Temptation becomes sin when we give into it. There is a saying often attributed to Martin Luther, "*You cannot stop the birds from flying over your head, but you can keep them from building a nest in your hair.*" Thoughts that spring up in your mind and visual temptations that appear before your eyes are inevitable. But you can choose not to act on these temptations.

As believers, we should be prepared for temptation and develop discernment to recognize patterns of temptation or times in which we are most vulnerable to temptation. Paul instructs us not to "*give the devil an opportunity.*"[47] We should not give him a foothold in our lives that would lead us into temptations that would overwhelm us and cause us to sin.

Proverbs says: "*Watch the path of your feet, and all your ways will be established. Do not turn to the right nor to the left; Turn your foot from evil.*"[48] Know that God is with you in the midst of temptation. Develop discernment in identifying areas of vulnerability so you can avoid falling into sin. God will reward you for patiently enduring testing and temptation.[49]

Let God help you with victory over temptation.

Chapter 34: Transformation

Hebrews 4:12 *For the word of God is living and active and sharper than any two-edged sword, and piercing as far as the division of soul and spirit, of both joints and marrow, and able to judge the thoughts and intentions of the heart.*

We need a spiritual transformation. This is the theme that runs throughout this book and study. We need God and His Word to transform us spiritually into His likeness. In this chapter, we will talk about the transformation. In the next chapter, we will talk about what the end result looks like.

Earlier dealing with our adversary and spiritual warfare, we learned a false view of the world can destroy our witness and even guarantee that we will be captive to the world's system. The antidote is God's Word, which is truth. The Bible teaches that it is "the word of truth" and that all its "commandments are truth."[50] Jesus in His prayer to the Father for His disciples said: "*Sanctify them in the truth; your word is truth.*"[51]

Consider for just a moment the various characteristics that are assigned to God's Word in Hebrews 4:12 listed above. It is living and active. It is sharper than any sword. It can judge the thought and intentions of our heart. That is why the Bible is a key resource in our spiritual transformation.

Let's look at another passage: "*All Scripture is inspired by God and profitable for teaching, for reproof, for correction, for training in righteousness; so that the man of God may be adequate, equipped for every good work.*"[52] The Bible claims to be inspired by God. Later, we will go into more detail about biblical inspiration. But this passage goes on to explain the value of Scripture in spiritual transformation. The Bible is profitable for teaching and correction. It is value in training us in righteousness. And once we have made truth of God's Word part of our lives we will be "equipped for every good work." We will be prepared for the tasks God has for us.

How do we make the Bible part of our spiritual life so that it can transform us? Here are a few action steps for you to take.

First, make an appointment with God's Word. Set a consistent time to study the Bible. This can be a time in which you read the Bible and read a commentary or daily devotional that will give you a greater understanding of God's Word.

Second, record what you learn. Keep a journal to reflect on what God is teaching you through His Word. You can also list prayers you are praying and answers to those prayers. Keeping a record can be an encouragement in your spiritual growth.

Third, reflect on what God is teaching you through His Word. The Bible is full of admonitions to meditate on God's Word. *"Do not let this Book of the Law depart from your mouth; meditate on it day and night, so that you may be careful to do everything written in it. Then you will be prosperous and successful."*[53] This is exactly what believers have done. *"I will meditate on all your works and consider all your mighty deeds."*[54] *"May the words of my mouth and the meditation of my heart be pleasing in your sight, O Lord, my Rock and my Redeemer."*[55]

Memorizing the Bible makes the sword readily available.

Another way to reflect on what God is teaching you is to memorize His Word. Paul wrote: *"Let the word of Christ richly dwell within you, with all wisdom teaching and admonishing one another with psalms and hymns and spiritual songs, singing with thankfulness in your hearts to God."*[56] Memorizing God's Word will guide you in His path[57] and help you to avoid temptation.[58]

Fourth, keep God's Word with you. Keep a copy of the Bible with you. It may be a physical Bible or it could be a digital Bible that you keep on you cell phone or computer. In the Old Testament, the king was instructed to keep God's Word with him. *"It shall be with him and he shall read it all the days of his life, that he may learn to fear the LORD his God, by carefully observing all the words of this law and these statutes."*[59]

You might post Bible verses in prominent places around your home. You might carry small cards of verses. You might listen to God's word on CD/mp3 while walking, exercising, or driving. This is a way to get God's Word into your heart, soul, and mind so the Bible is your "meditation all the day."[60]

Fifth, share God's word with others. Bring the Bible into your daily conversation with others. You can do this as you meet with people, but you could also text a key scripture verse to someone.

We can use the Bible in witnessing to others. Jesus told His disciples that *"you shall be My witnesses both in Jerusalem, and in all Judea and Samaria, and even to the remotest part of the earth."*[61] As we will see in a later chapter on witnessing and evangelism, the Bible is an important tool in sharing your faith.

We should also share God's Word with other Christians. Paul instructed Timothy that: *"The things which you have heard from me in the presence of many witnesses, entrust these to faithful men who will be able to teach others also."*[62] Sharing what God is teaching you through His Word and hearing from others what God is teaching them is another way to grow spiritually.

Finally, apply God's Word to your life. The Bible teaches that: *"The steps of a man are established by the Lord, And He delights in his way."*[63] Use God's Word in your spiritual walk and apply biblical principles to your life. Jesus taught that: *"everyone who hears these words of Mine and acts on them, may be compared to a wise man who built his house on the rock."*[64] Build your life on the solid rock of God's Word, and you will see spiritual transformation take place in your life.

Build your life on the solid rock of God's Word.

Chapter 35: Become Like Christ

Eph. 4:24 P*ut on the new self, which in the likeness of God has been created in righteousness and holiness of the truth.*

God wants us to become like Christ. And many Christians desire to become more Christ-like. Yet most Christians fall short of this desire. Spiritual growth isn't so much about "doing". It is more about "becoming" daily more like Christ. The Bible teaches God predestined us *"to become conformed to the image of His Son, so that He would be the firstborn among many brethren."*[65] And He promised to see the process through to the end.[66]

God created us in His image making us spiritual beings. We are eternal beings with some of the attributes of God. That doesn't mean we will be gods. That lie began in the Garden of Eden when Satan tempted Adam and Eve by saying *"you will be like God."*[67] It does mean that God sent His Son to earth to restore the full image we lost in the Fall. Jesus Christ gives us a clearer picture of the image of God. Jesus is described as being in *"the likeness of God."*[68] He is in *"the image of the invisible God."*[69] The *"whole fullness of deity dwells in Christ."*[70]

What are the steps to becoming more like Christ? First, we must surrender ourselves to God. As we present our bodies as "living sacrifices" to God, our minds are renewed and transformed.[71] The New Testament provides many examples of this surrender. When Jesus called Peter and Andrew to follow Him, they left their nets immediately.[72] Matthew, the tax collector, left his money tables immediately.[73] Paul encouraged believers to follow him as he follows Christ.[74]

We have been freed from sin. Jesus led a sinless life. We do not, but we should consider ourselves "dead to sin"[75] living a life of holiness.[76] Yes, we can still be tempted by sin and even fall into sin. But sin is no longer our master.[77] We can be victorious in our fight against temptation and sin by relying on God's

Word,[78] Christ's victory over sin,[79] and the power of the Holy Spirit in our lives.[80]

Becoming more Christ-like is a life-long process. As new Christians, we are immature spiritually. Paul admonishes these Christians to grow in Christ: *"We proclaim Him, admonishing every man and teaching every man with all wisdom, so that we may present every man complete in Christ."*[81] Peter says that we are to *"grow in the grace and knowledge of our Lord and Savior Jesus Christ."*[82]

Put on your new self; created in righteousness.

Ephesians says we should *"put on the new self, which in the likeness of God has been created in righteousness and holiness of the truth."*[83] Earlier in this letter, Paul puts this process in perspective. First, he gives us a vision of growing up in Christ:

> *And He gave some as . . . evangelists, and some as pastors and teachers, for the equipping of the saints for the work of service, to the building up of the body of Christ; until we all attain. . . to a mature man . . . As a result, we are no longer to be children, tossed here and there by waves and carried about by every wind of doctrine, by the trickery of men, by craftiness in deceitful scheming; but speaking the truth in love, we are to grow up in all aspects into Him who is the head, even Christ.*[84]

We are not to be childlike easily deceived by every new doctrine. When we are mature, God can use us in unimaginable ways. Paul reminds us to no longer act like the Gentiles:

> *Walk no longer just as the Gentiles also walk, in the futility of their mind, being darkened in their understanding, excluded from the life of God because of the ignorance that is in them, because of the hardness of their heart;*[85]

Even though we are not to think or act like non-believers, we have seen previously that isn't always the case with Christians in America. Paul talks about this present reality. Becoming Christ-like is a life-long process of spiritual growth:

lay aside the old self, which is being corrupted in accordance with the lusts of deceit, and that you be renewed in the spirit of your mind, and put on the new self, which in the likeness of God has been created in righteousness and holiness of the truth.[86]

To become more like Christ, we depend on the Holy Spirit. Relying on the Spirit, we *"are being transformed into his image with ever-increasing glory, which comes from the Lord, who is the Spirit."*[87] This process is sanctification. The Holy Spirit empowers change into the likeness of Christ; *"it is God who is at work in you, both to will and to work for His good pleasure."*[88]

We, however, must cooperate with the Holy Spirit and be willing to change. First, we must do our part stepping out in faith. At least eight times in the New Testament, we are instructed to "make every effort." Second, we must develop the mind of Christ. Paul teaches the need to renew our minds in his letter to Roman Christians.[89] He also talks about being "renewed in the spirit of your mind" in the passage from Ephesians.[90] Third, we should also "put on the new self" which means we must "put on" the character of Jesus Christ.

When we strive to become more like Him, we will be fulfilled because we are obeying Him. But we will also become a positive example for Christianity. In fact, one of the most significant benefits to becoming like Christ can be found in evangelism. Our public testimony of faith will attract others to Jesus Christ.

John Stott tells of the impact Christians could make if they lived more authentic lives. "There was a Hindu professor in India who said to a Christian student: "If you Christians lived like Jesus Christ, India would be at your feet tomorrow." I think India would be at their feet today if we Christians lived like Christ. From the Islamic world, the Reverend Iskandar Jadeed, a former Arab Muslim, has said "If all Christians were Christians – that is, Christ-like – there would be no more Islam today."[91]

As we strive to be like Christ, we are examples to others.

Chapter 36: Renewed Mind Transforms Life

Rom. 12:1-2 *Therefore I urge you, brethren, by the mercies of God, to present your bodies a living and holy sacrifice, acceptable to God, which is your spiritual service of worship. And do not be conformed to this world, but be transformed by the renewing of your mind, so that you may prove what the will of God is, that which is good and acceptable and perfect.*

God wants to transform us through a renewed mind. In this chapter, we return to the topic of spiritual transformation by focusing on how the Bible can accomplish this. No doubt you have had times when you have given your sins to the Lord and found they returned within minutes or hours. Why do we seem to constantly battle temptation? Can the Bible and the Holy Spirit help us to be victorious in this battle? Yes, but we need to know how to be transformed by God's Word as described above.

What does Paul mean when he says we should be transformed? The Greek "metamorphoo," means to change into another form. It is the root word from which we get our English word "metamorphosis." That is what happens to a caterpillar when it turns into a butterfly. God doesn't want us to remain spiritual caterpillars but become spiritual butterflies. It is worth noting that the Bible uses this same Greek word to describe what happened to Jesus on the Mount of Transfiguration.[1] This was a significant spiritual transformation that took place before the disciples. Likewise, our spiritual transformation through renewing our minds is to be a significant event in our lives.

What Paul is saying is that we should become new creatures. In fact, that is how he describes spiritual transformation in his letter to the Corinthians: "*Therefore if any man is in Christ, he is a new creature; the old things are passed away; behold, new things have come.*"[2] What is the goal of this transformation? We just discussed this in the previous chapter. We are to become like Christ. Earlier in Romans, Paul said that we are "*to become conformed to the image of His Son."*[3] He also says that we are *"being transformed into the same image"* of Christ.[4]

How does this transformation take place? There are a number of steps. The first is to learn from God's Word. There are thousands of self-help books on the market, but only the Bible can truly change you from the inside out and help you become what God intends for your life. The Holy Spirit cannot transform us until we have knowledge from God's Word of what He intends for us. Our mind cannot be renewed on a starvation diet rarely reading God's Word. Our mind cannot be renewed on a junk-food diet filling our minds with immoral images from television. We should feast on God's Word.

Your mind will not be renewed on a junk food diet.

Not only reading God's Word, but meditating on it. *"Do not let this Book of the Law depart from your mouth; meditate on it day and night, so that you may be careful to do everything written in it. Then you will be prosperous and successful."*[5] Use biblical study to bring God's principles into your life. Declare war on unbiblical and immoral thoughts dwelling in your mind.

In essence, you need a biblical mindset. Paul instructs us to *"Set your mind on the things above, not on the things that are on earth."*[6] You need to set your mind on spiritual things and not be conformed to this world and its patterns of thought. By doing so, you develop right thinking in the Lord.

Second, apply the principle of replacement, a two-fold process of "putting away" certain things and "putting on" other things. You must "put away" the immoral things that tempt you to sin. And you must also "put on" the godly qualities that God teaches in His Word. We cannot merely remove evil from our lives and expect to be successful as Christians. We must replace it with that which is good. Push out the sinful thought patterns with Scriptural truth. This is the principle of replacement.

In the Probe Ministries survey, we asked about 25 sinful activities and found the majority of born-again, young adults believed these behaviors to be wrong and usually felt guilty or embarrassed if they engaged in them.[95] They admitted they did not have victory over these various sins and behaviors.

If anger is your problem, you need to "put away" your bad temper and "put on" self-control. If lying is your problem, you need to "put away" dishonesty and "put on" honesty and integrity. If pornography is your problem, you need to "put away" lust and "put on" purity.

How do we do this effectively? We must declare war on wrong thoughts and emotions. Begin the day spending time in God's Word. As you read, meditate, and memorize, the Holy Spirit will use the Word to renew your mind. Your negative thought patterns can be replaced by biblical principles of the Word of God. The key difference between worldliness and godliness is a renewed mind under the control of the Holy Spirit.

Spiritual transformation through a renewed mind is a partnership with the Holy Spirit. We do our part by studying God's Word and apply the principle of replacement. But we must also depend upon the power of the Holy Spirit. Paul ends Romans with these words: *"Now may the God of hope fill you with all joy and peace in believing, so that you will abound in hope by the power of the Holy Spirit."*[7]

Finally, pay attention to temptation. Christians will always feel temptation as long as they live in this world. Temptation is not sin, but it can lead to sin. It is a call to action; an alarm system alerting us to the spiritual battle. To be victorious, we must ensure our thoughts are not *"conformed to this world,"* but *"transformed by the renewing of your mind."*

To live new, your mind must be renewed.

 10/30

Chapter 37: Renewed Mind and Discernment

Rom. 12:2 *not be conformed to this world, but be transformed by the renewing of your mind, so that you may prove what the will of God is, that which is good and acceptable and perfect.*

When spiritual transformation takes place, it affects the way we view the world and the way we live. Thinking according to biblical principles should lead to living by biblical principles.

As discussed in prior chapters, there is good evidence that Christians are not thinking or living biblically. Surveys show that less than one-third of young adults are born-again. Of these born-again Christians, one-third had a biblical worldview. That means they had orthodox views on six questions about God, Jesus, salvation, morality, Satan and the Bible.

When these born-again Christians with a biblical worldview were asked six additional questions, the numbers dropped once again. These six questions were about the uniqueness of Jesus, science, sharing their faith, world religions, their purpose in life, and the accuracy of the Bible. Only half of these born-again Christians with a biblical worldview could answer these questions in a manner consistent with the Bible.

These disturbing findings remind us that Christians are not very effective in following biblical teaching but instead accept the views of the culture. Paul warned Christians in the first century that they should *"not be conformed to this world, but be transformed by the renewing of your mind, so that you may prove what the will of God is, that which is good and acceptable and perfect."*[8]

Put another way, we need to develop discernment not being conformed to this world as worldly Christians. Many biblical passages call for believers to exercise discernment. Solomon prayed for discernment: *"So give Your servant an understanding heart to judge Your people to discern between good and evil. For who is able to judge this great people of Yours?"*[9]

The book of Proverbs encourages use to seek wisdom and discernment:

> *My son, if you will receive my words and treasure my commandments within you, Make your ear attentive to wisdom, incline your heart to understanding; For if you cry for discernment, lift your voice for understanding; If you seek her as silver and search for her as for hidden treasures; Then you will discern the fear of the Lord and discover the knowledge of God.*[10]

Paul prayed "*that your love may abound still more and more in real knowledge and all discernment, so that you may approve the things that are excellent, in order to be sincere and blameless until the day of Christ.*"[11] John taught that we should "*not believe every spirit, but test the spirits to see whether they are from God, because many false prophets have gone out into the world.*"[12] The writer of Hebrews reminds us "*solid food is for the mature, who because of practice have their senses trained to discern good and evil.*"[13] When we have discernment, our senses will be trained so that we can distinguish between good and evil.

Use biblical standards not cultural standards

When we exercise discernment, we choose biblical standards that honor God rather than cultural standards. In order to free ourselves from cultural captivity, we need to be transformed by the renewing of our minds so that we are not conformed to the culture. That was true in Paul's day, and it is certainly true in our day with the powerful cultural influences broadcast through the media. We live in a decadent, sexualized, materialistic culture. If we are to live for Christ, we must live counter-culturally to these pervasive influences.

John warns us of the three categories of things in this world that can seduce us and conform us to the culture:

> *Do not love the world nor the things in the world. If anyone loves the world, the love of the Father is not in him. For all that is in the world, the lust of the flesh and the lust of the eyes and the boastful pride of life, is not from the Father, but is from the world. The world is passing away, and also its lusts; but the one who does the will of God lives forever.*[14]

The "lust of the flesh" is easily seen in our sexualized culture. It includes everything from sexual images on television to pornography on the Internet. Paul commands us to walk in the Spirit and not by the lust of the flesh.[15] The "lust of the eyes" is seen in advertising that encourages our greed and materialism. Jesus tells us to beware of covetousness.[16] And the "pride of life" is seen in the narcissism of our society and how pride causes us to make wrong decisions. The book of Proverbs warns that pride can lead to shame,[17] strife,[18] and destruction.[19]

A wise, discerning Christian always asks whether an activity (watching a TV program, listening to music, visiting certain websites) is what God desires for us. Years ago, Christians wore a WWJD bracelet -- What would Jesus do? First, we need discernment to evaluate what we are doing. Second, we need courage to follow biblical commands and principles and refrain from that which is harmful to us and those around us.

Paul warns: *"Therefore be careful how you walk, not as unwise men but as wise, making the most of your time, because the days are evil."*[20] We should heed his warning and make sure we are living in righteousness. We need discernment to make right choices so our lives are not filled with things that hinder our Christian walk and grieve the heart of God.

Discernment to evaluate and courage to act in response to God's leading is key.

Chapter 38: The Bible is God's Truth

2 Tim. 3:16 *All Scripture is inspired by God and profitable for teaching, for reproof, for correction, for training in righteousness; so that the man of God may be adequate, equipped for every good work.*

If you want to know how to effectively use an appliance or an electronic device, it is wise to consult the owner's manual. The Bible is the manual for our Christian faith. It is where we learn about the character of God and the story of salvation.

Paul writes to Timothy: *"All Scripture is inspired by God and profitable for teaching, for reproof, for correction, for training in righteousness; so that the man of God may be adequate, equipped for every good work."*[21] What does Paul mean when he says that the Bible is "inspired"? The Greek word used here means "God breathed." In other words, God has breathed His instructions to us into His Word, which was recorded by the human authors of the books in the Bible.

God has given us His Word so that we might believe. But He has also given it to us so that we might teach, reprove, correct, and train. First, we are to teach. But in order to teach biblical truth, we must know biblical truth. This requires that we study the Word of God. In previous chapters we talked about the importance of reading the Bible daily, attending church and Bible study, and studying the foundational doctrines of the Christian faith.

Second, we are to reprove others. When we see others violating biblical commands and engaging in sinful practices, we should not ignore their behavior. Later on in his letter to Timothy, Paul adds that he is to *"preach the word; be ready in season and out of season; reprove, rebuke, exhort, with great patience and instruction."*[22] We are to warn others of sin. Our warnings may be to a young believer who is not aware of sin or to a mature believer who is ignoring God's warnings in Scripture.

Third, we are to correct others. That means we are to restore others by correcting their unbiblical doctrine or their immoral actions. The Word of God is our standard for doctrine and behavior. Paul teaches that *"if anyone is caught in any trespass, you who are spiritual, restore such a one in a spirit of gentleness; each one looking to yourself, so that you too will not be tempted."*[23]

Finally, we are to train others in righteousness. This includes education in the home (training and educating children) and in the church (training believers). We must hear the Word; we must study the Word; and we must apply the Word.

As believers, we should accept the authority of the Word of God. James teaches that: *"Every good and perfect gift is from above, coming down from the Father of the heavenly lights, who does not change like shifting shadows. He chose to give us birth through the word of truth, that we might be a kind of first fruits of all he created."*[24] The Bible should be our standard for doctrine and behavior, because we are reading the Word of God. The book of Proverbs teaches that: *"every word of God is flawless."*[25]

The Bible is our standard for doctrine and behavior.

Although Christians should accept the authority and reliability of the Bible, we have discovered that this emerging generation of believers have many questions about the Bible and may even doubt its accuracy.

The Probe Ministries survey examined the perspective of born-again, young adults on the Bible.[95] Seven out of ten born-again adults say they take the Bible as the source of truth and that it applies to all situations and all people. As you might imagine, the percentage was higher for those with a biblical worldview than for those without a biblical worldview.

Six out of ten born-again adults believe the statement "everything the Bible says is true when interpreted correctly" is true for everyone. While a quarter think this statement is true for them but not for everyone.

Born-again adults were all across the board when it comes to their thoughts on the Bible and science. One third thought that the statement "the Bible and science are essentially consistent" was true for everyone. Others felt the statement was true for me but not for others or not true for them but may be for others or not true for anyone.

The results of this survey should concern us. This generation of born-again adults does not always hold the Bible in the same esteem as previous generations. In the following chapters, we will look at some of the evidence for the authority and reliability of the Bible. This evidence should increase our confidence in God's Word and equip each of us to share it with others. We can know that *"the word of the Lord is right and true."*[26]

The Bible is truth in everything it addresses.

Chapter 39: Biblical Inspiration

2 Peter 1:20 *No prophecy of scripture ever comes about by the prophet's own imagination, for no prophecy was ever borne of human impulse; rather, men carried along by the Holy Spirit spoke from God.*

Why should Christians believe in the authority and inspiration of the Bible? It is true that the Bible claims to be the Word of God.[27] But it is a circular argument to say that the Bible proves it is the Word of God merely because it claims to be the Word of God. It is, however, a necessary starting point.

Since the Bible claims to be the Word of God, let's see if there is any evidence that it is indeed God's Word. First, let's look at what the Bible claims about itself. In the Old Testament, we read claims that God has spoken to His people.[28] The Bible says that the nation of Israel was established by the spoken and written Word of God.[29] The prophets were told to write down what God said.[30]

In the New Testament, we see that Jesus bore witness to the Old Testament.[31] And His apostles bore witness to the Old Testament.[32] Jesus also claimed to be speaking the words of the Father.[33] And He told the disciples that the Spirit would bring to remembrance all He had taught them.[34]

The Bible and the people in the Bible make some very dramatic claims about the Bible. Do we have any evidence that it is more than merely the writings of some Hebrew prophets? We can see evidence of Divine fingerprints in Scripture because of its fulfilled prophecy and historical accuracy.

When the Bible was written, more than one fourth of its content was prophetic in nature. Many of these prophecies have been fulfilled, and this provides strong evidence of the Divine nature of Scripture. In the Old Testament, we have prophecies about various people and kingdoms before they ever existed.

There are prophecies about 737 separate matters that are predicted in the Bible.[35]

Fulfilled prophecy validates the Bible. If these prophecies can be verified as accurate, then we can assume that other things that we cannot verify (attributes of God, heaven, grace, salvation) must also be accurate. The Bible records events before they happen. Prophecy is history written in advance.

The most persuasive collection of prophecies is about the coming Messiah. These were Messianic prophecies written down in the Old Testament that were literally fulfilled in the life, death, burial, and resurrection of Jesus Christ. Biblical scholars have catalogued 332 prophecies that were all fulfilled by Jesus.[36]

332 biblical prophecies fulfilled by the life of Jesus.

The Old Testament predicts the lineage of the Messiah.[37] The prophet Micah predicted that the Messiah would be born in the small town of Bethlehem.[38] Zechariah says that the Messiah will enter Jerusalem riding a donkey.[39] Zechariah also predicts that a friend will betray him, for thirty pieces of silver, which would be cast in the Temple, and then used to buy a potter's field.[40] Other prophecies predict that he will be pierced and those around him will cast lots for his clothing.[41] Isaiah says he would be numbered with transgressors (criminals) and buried with the rich.[42]

What are the mathematical odds that all of these prophecies could be fulfilled by chance or by manipulation? Professor Peter Stoner was chairman of the Department of Mathematics and Astronomy at Pasadena City College for many years before he became professor of science at Westmont College. He calculated these probabilities in his book, *Science Speaks: Scientific Proof of the Accuracy of Prophecy and the Bible.* He concluded that the probability of one person fulfilling just eight of these messianic prophecies was 1 in 10 to the 17th power. The probability of fulfilling 48 prophecies was 1 in 10 to the 157th power.[43]

The Bible also is historically accurate and in accord with the facts of history, culture, and science. In the next chapter we will examine in further detail the reliability of the Bible. But here we should acknowledge that the Bible gives names of people and places along with dates that can be verified historically. History and archaeology verify the accuracy of the Bible. And though the Bible is not a scientific textbook, it also makes statements that are in accord with science. Unlike what some people say, you do not have to deny science to accept the truth of the Bible.

Whole books have been written about the inspiration and accuracy of the Bible. A serious student can investigate the claims of the Bible and observe the Divine nature of Scripture. We do not have doubt in the inspiration of the Bible. It provides "many convincing proofs."[44]

Many serious students have started out to prove the Bible is false and have ended up affirming it as true.

Chapter 40: Biblical Reliability

1 Pet. 3:15 *always being ready to make a defense to everyone who asks you to give an account for the hope that is in you, yet with gentleness and reverence;*

Why should Christians believe in the reliability of the Bible? Through the centuries skeptics have attacked the historical accuracy and reliability of the Bible. Do we have good reasons to trust the Bible? Let's look at the internal evidence and the external evidence for the reliability of the New Testament.

Critics claim that the Gospels were written after the lifetimes of the eyewitnesses. Therefore, they argue, much of what we read in the Gospels about Jesus is myth and legend. They suggest that the Jesus of history has been embellished into the Christ of faith. In other words, they argue, we really don't have an accurate picture of Jesus in the Gospels and don't have an accurate record of events in the New Testament.

There are good reasons to reject the idea that the New Testament was written much later than the first century. For example, three of the Gospels prophesied the fall of the Jerusalem Temple. We know that occurred in A.D. 70. None of the Gospels (or any other part of the New Testament) even mentions the destruction of the Temple. The most plausible explanation is that its destruction had not occurred at the time when the New Testament was written.

New Testament scholars give strong evidence that the New Testament was completed in the first century (by A.D. 100).[45] That means that the New Testament was written by eyewitnesses. This fact alone contradicts the idea that there is the Jesus of history and then a later Christ of faith. There is a connection between the two.[46]

The letters of Paul and Peter were obviously written before their deaths (during the Neronian persecution in A.D. 64). It is worth noting that the book of Acts not only does not record the destruction of the Temple, but it does not record the death of the two chief characters: Paul and Peter. Instead, the book ends with Paul living under house arrest. The most plausible explanation is that Luke finished writing the book of Acts before these historical events took place. These and many other facts point to an early date for the Gospels and the rest of the New Testament.

What about the external evidence for the reliability of the Bible? New Testament scholars have an enormous amount of documentary evidence. In fact, this evidence far surpasses any other work of antiquity. There are over 5,000 Greek manuscripts alone, and many are dated within years of the lives of the authors. There are also Latin manuscripts, and manuscripts of other languages (Coptic, Armenian, Syriac). These manuscripts helped missionaries in the first few centuries reach new cultures with the Gospel in their own language. When you add up all of these manuscripts of the New Testament, the number is more than 25,000 and far exceeds the manuscript evidence for any other piece of literature from antiquity.

Modern technology and recent findings increase our confidence in the accuracy of the biblical text.

Using modern technology to help read the contents of ancient documents found in mummy bindings, old buildings, and other unusual places, the number of portions of ancient New Testaments being found is continuing to increase. These new finding are increasing our confidence in the accurate process of manuscript production.

It is also worth mentioning that the early church fathers (Clement, Polycarp, etc.) quoted from the New Testament as they wrote to each other. All together there are well over 38,000 quotations from the New Testament, which provide further confirmation of the biblical text.

Further external confirmation of the reliability of the Bible comes from history and archaeology. Extra-biblical historical accounts confirm facts and dates in the Bible. Archaeology verifies the accuracy of biblical accounts in both the Old Testament and the New Testament.

In the past, skeptics attacked the historical accuracy of Luke (author of the Gospel of Luke and the book of Acts). Archaeologist Sir William Ramsay, for example, was skeptical of the historical nature of the New Testament. But when he studied the dates, places, and people in the book of Acts he discovered that it was "an authority for the topography, antiquities, and society of Asia Minor. It was gradually borne in upon me that in various details the narrative showed marvelous truth."[47]

Luke names key historical figures in the correct time sequence as well as correct titles to government officials in various areas. One scholar concludes that: "Luke names thirty-two countries, fifty-four cities, and nine islands without error."[48]

Whole books have been written about the reliability of the Bible. You should take the time to study the abundant evidence for biblical reliability. It will strengthen and encourage your faith and provide you with effective arguments as you share your faith with others. Your study will enable you to be "*ready to make a defense . . . for the hope that is in you.*"[49]

The abundant evidence for biblical reliability will strengthen and encourage your faith.

Chapter 41: Biblical Application

Acts 20:32 *I commend you to God and to the word of His grace, which is able to build you up and to give you the inheritance among all those who are sanctified.*

It is not enough that we read the Bible and believe the Bible. We should apply biblical instruction and commands to our life. The Bible is much more than a collection of doctrines. It is an instrument God uses to transform our lives.

In his farewell message to the believers in Ephesus, Paul reminds them that God's Word can build them up and transform their lives. *"I commend you to God and to the word of His grace, which is able to build you up and to give you the inheritance among all those who are sanctified."*[50]

Peter encourages us to use God's Word in our lives because it contains what we need to be transformed. *"His divine power has granted to us everything pertaining to life and godliness, through the true knowledge of Him who called us by His own glory and excellence. For by these He has granted to us His precious and magnificent promises, so that by them you may become partakers of the divine nature, having escaped the corruption that is in the world by lust."*[51]

God desires that we live a life of godliness. We are to be holy as He is holy.[52] We are to be perfect as God is perfect.[53] Peter is telling us that God has provided all that is necessary so that we might be enabled to live a life that is holy and full of virtue.

The Word of God will cleanse us. Jesus taught: *"You are already clean because of the word which I have spoken to you."*[54] And he taught that we can be sanctified by God's Word because His Word is truth.[55] We can live a pure life by following God's Word: *"How can a young man keep his way pure? By keeping it according to your word."*[56] God has provided His promises to us so that we can become partakers of the divine nature.

In order for God's Word to work in our lives, we must do a number of things. First, we should accept the authority of God's Word. James reminds us that; *"Every good thing given and every perfect gift is from above, coming down from the Father of lights, with whom there is no variation or shifting shadow. In the exercise of His will He brought us forth by the word of truth, so that we would be a kind of first fruits among His creatures."*[57]

We live in a fallen world that is tempting us to listen to other voices vying for our attention and asking us to accept their authority. We are told to base our decisions on majority opinion ("everyone is doing it") or on human tradition ("that's the way we have always done it") or upon human reason ("it seemed the right thing to do").

No other source of authority can match the Bible as a standard of truth for living.

In the study Probe Ministries commissioned of born-again, young adults, there was a striking difference between those who accepted the Bible as their final authority and those who did not. They were asked how their personal behavior aligned with what the Bible says about many of the moral topics we surveyed. Those with a biblical worldview scored themselves significantly higher than those without a biblical worldview.[95]

The Bible reminds us that, *"every word of God is flawless."*[58] Paul teaches us that God's inspired Word is *"profitable for teaching, for reproof, for correction, for training in righteousness."*[59]

Second, we must make God's Word part of our lives. Jesus instructed us to *"abide in Him"* because a *"branch cannot bear fruit of itself unless it abides in the vine, so neither can you unless you abide in Me."*[60] We do this through the study of God's Word, which provides spiritual nourishment to us. Notice that the Bible is called our pure milk,[61] our bread,[62] and solid food.[63]

Finally, we must apply the Word of God to our lives. James warns against believers who are only hearers of the Word and not doers of the Word.[64] Part of this involves thinking biblically about life and developing the "mind of Christ" as we discussed in previous chapters. But it also involves more than our minds. It involves our will. We must apply these biblical truths to our lives.

We must build our lives upon the solid foundation of God's Word. Jesus said, *"Everyone who hears these words of Mine and acts on them, may be compared to a wise man who built his house on the rock."*[65]

Your life and your character are like a house. Every thought and every action are the wood and stone that is building various parts of your house. You can build your house on a firm foundation and follow God's blueprint in constructing the house. Or you can build on an unstable foundation and construct the rooms of your house based upon your whims or the influence of the world.

If Jesus is a foundation,[66] we will not be swept away in the flood of immorality currently inundating the world. We will not be destroyed by the trials of life that flood into our lives on a regular basis. If our foundation is firm and our building strong, we will be able to withstand the trials and temptations of the world.

Paul reminds us: *"God's solid foundation stands firm."*[67] Build your life on the solid foundation of God's Word.

With a firm foundation of God's Word, we are able to stand strong in this world.

Chapter 42: Prayer

Col. 4:2 *Devote yourselves to prayer, keeping alert in it with an attitude of thanksgiving*

Just as the Bible is the foundation of our Christian walk, so also is prayer an integral part of the Christian life. As noted above, Paul instructed the Colossians to devote themselves to prayer. Prayer is our pipeline to God. It is how we communicate with Him, and how He can lead us daily in our Christian walk. He can channel His instructions and His blessings to us through prayer.

Jesus taught us that the heavenly Father is waiting for us to pray to Him and ready to answer our requests. Near the end of His Sermon on the Mount, Jesus taught his disciples this about prayer:

> *"Ask, and it will be given to you; seek, and you will find; knock, and it will be opened to you.*
> *For everyone who asks receives, and he who seeks finds,*
> *and to him who knocks it will be opened.*
> *Or what man is there among you who,*
> *when his son asks for a loaf, will give him a stone?*
> *Or if he asks for a fish, he will not give him a snake, will he?*
> *If you then, being evil, know how to give good gifts*
> *to your children,*
> *how much more will your Father who is in heaven give what is good to those who ask Him!"*[68]

Jesus is telling us that God is eagerly waiting to give us what we need and request from Him. He has given us incredible access to him. He has opened the door to heaven and is ready to provide for us. In fact, Paul says that God *"is able to do far more abundantly beyond all that we ask or think."*[69]

Notice the progression in the words Jesus used: ask, seek, and knock. When we ask for something that is stronger than not asking. When we seek, we are taking action. That verb is even stronger than the verb to ask. Then Jesus says we are to knock. That is even stronger, because we are knocking at the door to heaven. We are imploring the God of the universe to answer our prayers. Jesus also taught that when *"you ask in prayer, believing, you will receive."*[70]

What happens when we don't pray? If we neglect prayer in our Christian life, we limit what God might do in our lives or in the lives of other people. God certainly is omniscient (He knows our needs) and omnipotent (He can do all things). But he is waiting for us to pray to him. James says: *"You do not have because you do not ask."*[71] He also reminds us that, *"Every good thing given and every perfect gift is from above, coming down from the Father of lights, with whom there is no variation or shifting shadow."*[72]

Don't limit God's work in and through your life. Pray!

Jesus provided a model for prayer in his life. The Bible records that Jesus went up on a mountain to pray[73] and that he often withdrew into the wilderness to pray.[74] In one of the most poignant images of prayer, we see that before he was crucified, Jesus was in the garden of Gethsemane. He withdrew from the disciples to pray.[75]

Paul's life also provides a model for prayer. Often in his letters, he asked other Christians to pray for him. He asked them to pray that God would give him the right words when he spoke.[76] He asked that they pray that God would open a door for his ministry.[77] And he also prayed for these Christians, that their love would abound[78] and that God would strengthen them.[79]

We also see the importance of prayer in the lives of the early Christians. The Bible says that they continued steadfastly in prayer[80] and that they devoted themselves continually to prayer.[81] They prayed when church leaders were selected[82] and when missionaries were sent out.[83]

These testimonies of prayer should encourage us to pray. We can also gain encouragement to pray when we look at all the ministry achievements the Bible explains will be accomplished through prayer.

Here is a short list of things God does through our prayers:

1. Prayer is a way to strengthen Christians.[84]
2. Prayer is a way to defeat Satan.[85]
3. Prayer is how we help save those who are lost.[86]
4. Prayer is how we get more Christians into the mission field.[87]
5. Prayer is how we gain knowledge of His will.[88]
6. Prayer is how we can gain wisdom.[89]
7. Prayer is how we can learn not to be anxious.[90]
8. Prayer is how we can restore a person who has fallen into sin.[91]

God has chosen to do most of His work in our lives through prayer. That is why prayer is so important and why Paul admonished believers to "*pray without ceasing.*"[92] Have you prayed today?

If we are to be God's representative on this earth, we must check in with Him through prayer.

Chapter 43: The Church

Hebrews 10:24-25 *Let us consider how to stimulate one another to love and good deeds, not forsaking our own assembling together, as is the habit of some, but encouraging one another;*

The Christian life was not meant to be lived alone. God intends for us to be part of His family of believers. You were created as an essential part of this family. The church is where believers gather regularly to worship, to learn about Him and the Christian life, and to bring the gospel to the world.

Jokes about attending "the church of the inner springs" and "bedside Baptists" say it really doesn't matter whether a Christian attends church regularly. This perspective is justified by saying we are part of the worldwide, universal church and don't need a local church. We are part of the body of Christ,[1] and are admonished to gather together with other believers.[2]

The parts of a computer are not a functioning computer until all are connected. You might have a monitor, a keyboard, and the processor, but you don't have a functioning computer unless these parts are connected. Likewise, the church must be together if it is going to fulfill God's purpose for it in the world. The primary reason to attend church is to obey God and please Him. Being actively involved in a church is vital for our spiritual wellbeing. Now, the elderly or disabled may only be able to participate in church remotely. That is not justification for able-bodied Christians to avoid connecting with other believers.

You may have had a bad experience in church and not want to try another. That is understandable given the fact that spiritual abuse sometimes does take place in churches with an authoritarian structure or churches that are very legalistic. While that may be a reason not to attend that particular church, it is not a good reason to avoid a different gathering of believers. The New Testament writers never divided the body into attenders and non-attenders. They assumed believers would participate in their local assembly. While some Christians were isolated by geography, the norm was believers meeting together. In a new area, Paul would win a few converts and quickly start a church. Here are some reasons why having a church and being involved is important.

1. Worship – attending church is a visible expression of our love for God. When we gather together, we can worship the Lord corporately.[3] We can worship Him for who He is and what He is doing in our lives. Worship was important in the Old Testament. Psalm 100 calls for believers to: "*Worship the LORD with gladness; come before him with joyful songs.*"[4] And corporate worship is an important function of the New Testament church. Jesus says to worship God in Spirit and Truth.[5] Obviously, we can do that individually, but we are also called to gather together as believers.[6] And Paul says that we should be "*speaking to one another in psalms and hymns and spiritual songs, singing and making melody with your heart to the Lord.*"[7]

2. Obedience – Going to church is a matter of obedience. Hebrews tells us not to forsake assembling together.[8] We benefit from meeting with other believers. This fellowship will "*encourage (provoke, stimulate) love and good works.*" As believers we need to be encouraged, provoked, and stimulated. That is what attending a Bible-teaching church does for us.

3. Accountability – The Christian life is not lived alone, but in community; in obedience to those in spiritual leadership over us. Hebrews says : "*Obey your leaders and submit to them, for they are keeping watch over your souls, ... Let them do this with joy and not with groaning, for that would be of no advantage to you.*"[9] God designed a system of spiritual accountability inside the church to protect the body and also provide encouragement to grow in their faith. The church provides a foundation for spiritual growth through pastors, elders, deacons, and other leaders.

Peter instructs these leaders to watch over us as a shepherd. *"So I exhort the elders among you, . . . shepherd the flock of God that is among you, exercising oversight, not under compulsion, but willingly, as God would have you; not for shameful gain, but eagerly; not domineering over those in your charge, but being examples to the flock."*[10] Paul tells us to obey and esteem those in spiritual leadership over us. *"We ask you, brothers, to respect those who labor among you and are over you in the Lord and admonish you, and to esteem them very highly in love because of their work."*[11]

4. Ministry to the body – The church is a body in which each part is to use its gifts.[12] In doing this, we bring the good news to the world and minister to each other's needs and weaknesses. The Bible is filled with "one another" commands. We are to love one another[13] and accept one another.[14] We are to offer hospitality to one another.[15] We are to confess our sins to and pray for one another.[16] We are to comfort and encourage one another.[17,18] These actions take place in the community of the church.

5. Fellowship – Christians need a vertical relationship with God but also a horizontal relationship with other believers. Jesus told us the greatest commandment: *"You shall love the Lord your God with all your heart, . . . This is the great and foremost commandment. The second is like it, You shall love your neighbor as yourself."*[19]

It is not possible to love God and not also love others. We should not have an unforgiving spirit toward others.[20] You cannot say you are in the light when you hate another person. But *"he who loves his brother abides in the light."*[21] Attending church is not optional for a believer. It is necessary for our spiritual well-being and a vital part of our Christian walk.

Church fellowship is essential for our Christian walk.

Chapter 44: Body of Christ

1st Cor. 12:12 *For even as the body is one and yet has many members, and all the members of the body, though they are many, are one body, so also is Christ.*

The moment someone is born again, he or she becomes part of the body of Christ. In the previous chapter, we learned the importance of attending church and becoming united with fellow believers in the local church. In this chapter, we want to explore what it means to become part of the body of Christ.

At conversion you are born into the family of God. In many ways, your spiritual family is even more important than your physical family because your relationship to Christ and other believers will last for eternity. A major theme that runs through this book is the need for us as believers to live for eternity. God's family is a forever family that lasts for eternity.

When Jesus was told that his mother and brothers were outside wanting to speak to Him, He stretched His hand toward His disciples and said, "*Behold My mother and My brothers! For whoever does the will of My Father who is in heaven, he is My brother and sister and mother.*"[22] The Bible teaches that Jesus "*makes people holy and those who are made holy are of the same family.*" That is why "*Jesus is not ashamed to call them brothers and sisters.*"[23]

The Bible refers to the church as the body of Christ[24] and also refers to her as the bride of Christ.[25] This demonstrates the special place that believers have in Christ's kingdom. It also reminds us that we should also value the body of Christ. We have both a vertical relationship with God and a horizontal relationship with other believers in the body. John reminds us that we are to love our brother: "*The one who says he is in the Light and yet hates his brother is in the darkness until now. The one who loves his brother abides in the Light and there is no cause for stumbling in him."*[26] Jesus said, *"By this all men will know that you are My disciples, if you have love for one another."*[27]

In God's family we are connected to each other. Paul writes: *"For just as we have many members in one body and all the members do not have the same function, so we, who are many, are one body in Christ, and individually members one of another."*[28] There are many members with different gifts and abilities, but we are all part of the body of Christ. As we use our gifts for Christ's service, we fulfill His mission through us on earth.

Use our gifts in Christ's body to fulfill His mission in this world.

Paul explains: *"For even as the body is one and yet has many members, and all the members of the body, though they are many, are one body, so also is Christ."*[29] Earlier in the passage, he elaborates. *"Now there are varieties of gifts, but the same Spirit. And there are varieties of ministries, and the same Lord. There are varieties of effects, but the same God who works all things in all persons."*[30] As we use our gift within the body of Christ, we bless the church and the world.

Notice how Paul describes the use of our gifts. He says we are *"fitted together"* and *"built together."*[31] He also describes us as *"fellow heirs"* and *"fellow members of the body,"* and *"fellow partakers of the promise in Christ Jesus through the gospel."*[32]

C.S. Lewis pointed out that the "very word *membership* is of Christian origin, but it has been taken over by the world and emptied of all meaning. In any book on logic you may see the expression 'members of a class.' It must be most emphatically stated that the items or particulars included in a homogeneous class are almost the reverse of what St. Paul meant by *members.*"[33] In our world today, we have lost the biblical concept of membership.

Certainly we should be a member of a local church, but Paul was talking about being a vital part of the living body of Christ. We are part of a bigger part of Christ's kingdom as members of His body. Jesus proclaimed to Peter that: *"I will build My church; and the gates of Hades will not overpower it."* The universal church will ultimately be victorious through Christ and we will live for eternity.

The New Testament has 59 "one another" or "each other" verses. There are many verses that command us to "love one another."[34] We are to "pray for each other."[35] We are also to "encourage each other"[36] and "encourage one another."[37] We should also forgive "each other"[38] and admonish "one another."[39] We are to be involved in the lives of other Christians not live as a hermit or recluse. We are part of a body of Christ where we are to be involved with one another.

As believers we will also receive a rich inheritance because we are part of the family of God. First, Paul promised believers that *"my God will supply all your needs according to His riches in glory in Christ Jesus."*[40] The Bible also promises that we will be completely changed to be like Christ[41] and transformed into His likeness.[42] That also means we will ultimately be freed from pain, suffering, and death.[43] We will also share in Christ's glory.[44] This is why Peter proclaimed that we were *"born again to a living hope through the resurrection of Jesus Christ from the dead, to obtain an inheritance which is imperishable and undefiled and will not fade away, reserved in heaven for you."*[45]

What a privilege it is to be part of the body of Christ. We are blessed to use our gifts and abilities for Him, and we have an unbelievable inheritance awaiting us in eternity when we have finished our work here on earth.

Focus on using our gifts to proclaim Christ now, as we wait for our inheritance in heaven.

Chapter 45: Evangelism

Matt. 28:19 *Go therefore and make disciples of all nations*

God has given you a story to share. He has done a work in your life, and expects you will share it. We should not only live in Christ, but we are also commanded to witness to others. Jesus said this to His disciples: *"You are the light of the world. . . . Let your light shine before men in such a way that they may see your good works, and glorify your Father who is in heaven."*[46]

Today, people are interested in spirituality. They may not have a good opinion of Christians, but they are interested in connecting with something or someone greater than them. They may not believe they are sinful and need a savior. But they may be attracted to us because we are a light shining in the darkness. Living a consistent, biblical lifestyle can be attractive to others.

We have the privilege of making an impact on individuals and thus on families and communities. If we are sensitive to their needs, our witness will be effective. But to be effective, people must actually see the light. We have talked about how we need to walk with Christ manifesting the truth of the gospel. Our lives testify to the truthfulness of the gospel to others. Perhaps you have heard the statement: "Be careful how you live. You may be the only Bible some people will ever read."

We are commanded to go and make disciples. Before Jesus left this earth, He said: *"Go therefore and make disciples of all the nations, baptizing them in the name of the Father and the Son and the Holy Spirit, teaching them to observe all that I commanded you; and lo, I am with you always, even to the end of the age."*[47] This passage is called "The Great Commission" and marks the beginning of the church. It is Christ's personal instruction to go into the world and make disciples of all nations. Over the centuries, dedicated Christians have taken the gospel throughout the world. We have incredible stories of God's faithfulness as they journeyed into remote areas and suffered incredible hardships. Many Christians faced intense persecution even dying for their faith. Christ's command is not just for missionaries. He has called for us to share the good news with those around us. We don't have to travel to a remote area to find those who have never accepted Christ's love. They are all around us. We are commanded to witness to them.

Are Christians witnessing to others? Various surveys have asked Christians if they have witnessed or shared their faith with someone in the last year. In general, more than half of evangelicals answer that they have done so. But, in the Probe Ministries survey of born-again, young adults, only one percent said they had witnessed in the last month.[95] But 85 percent agreed they should share their religious experience with others.

We are called to share; not to have all of the answers.

Why don't more Christians share their faith? Many Christians are intimidated and feel inadequate. They feel they need all the answers to a skeptic's questions before witnessing. If someone raises an objection, it is okay to admit you don't know while offering to find an answer. The Internet (e.g. probe.org) is full of material from Christian ministries that will help answer questions people may raise. There is value in reading books or taking a course so that you can become a confident ambassador for Christ.[48]

Peter writes that we should, *"sanctify Christ as Lord in your hearts, always being ready to make a defense to everyone who asks you to give an account for the hope that is in you, yet with gentleness and reverence."*[49] Our attitude of gentleness is also an important part of our witness to the world. Christ said "*You will be my witnesses*"[50] not "You will be my debaters or my theologians or my apologists." We should share what Christ has done in our lives and be willing to look for answers to someone's questions. Even experienced Christians face times when they have questions raised they had not considered.

In today's religious climate, it is important to be a good listener. Often we won't have all the answers. People want to be heard, and so being a good listener might be even more important than being a good talker. We can share our testimony and allow the other person to deal with our walk with Christ. It is often helpful in our conversation with others to ask questions. Many times Jesus used questions to challenge people to consider who He was or to reconsider what they believed to be true. You can become more effective in your witness by asking questions allowing the other person to consider the claims of Christ and to reconsider what they believe to be true.

Our world today is similar to the pluralistic world of the first century. The people believed in many gods and were hostile to the idea of one true God declaring all other gods are false. They took offense at the idea of Jesus being Lord of all. Today, we also face hostility because of the exclusive claims of Christ.

Facing hostility, we should seek to be a friend and learn what caused the hostile reaction. Sometimes it may be theological, but often it is emotional. Someone may be turned off because of a problem they had with a church in their past. We can learn from the early church's practice of kindness and hospitality and build a bridge of friendship with the unbeliever.

Often it is good to have a person explain who they think God is and what Christianity is. Many people have misconceptions about God, Jesus, the Bible, and salvation. By listening and providing true, biblical perspectives on these topics, you can clear up misconceptions and bring them closer to saving faith.

Finally, we should remember only God can open a person's heart to faith in Him. We are responsible for sharing the gospel, and leaving the results to God. Jesus said, *"No one can come to Me unless the Father who sent Me draws him."*[51] The pressure is off of us. God will not hold us accountable if others do not believe. He will hold us accountable to share with others. We are to sow the seed. He brings the harvest. Go and share your faith.

We sow the seed. God brings the harvest.

Chapter 46: Our Identity and Purpose

1st Peter 2:9 But *you are a chosen race, a royal priesthood, a holy nation, a people for God's own possession, so that you may proclaim the excellencies of Him who has called you out of darkness into His marvelous light;*

How does God see us, and what does He want to accomplish in our lives? Remember that Paul refers to us as "Christ's ambassadors."[52] An ambassador is someone who represents his or her own country by living in a foreign country. Likewise, we are to represent Christ while living in this world. In this chapter we will look at how Peter answers these questions.

Our goal in this Once Captive experience is to free Christians from cultural captivity building them into confident ambassadors for Christ. An ambassador who adopts the culture of the foreign country is no longer distinct and no longer truly represents his or her own country. A confident ambassador is able to live temporarily in a foreign country but never forgets he or she is representing another country.

What are some of the attributes of an ambassador for Christ? Peter gives us four important markers in the passage above. He starts by calling us a "chosen race." He begins the sentence with the word "but" contrasting Christians from unbelievers he was talking about in the previous verse. In other words, we are different and should act differently from non-Christians. The phrase "chosen race" is the same descriptive title that was used in the Old Testament to describe elect servants.[53] God has chosen us for ministry. The Greek word for "race" implies hereditary privilege. We have been brought into a divine family through the new birth sharing in the privileges of being a child of God.

Peter explains that we are also a "royal priesthood." He explained previously that we are "living stones" that are "built up as a spiritual house" that is also a royal house of a royal family.[54] The phrase "royal priesthood" is also found in the Old Testament.[55] Just as Israel was called to bring to the world the knowledge of the true God, we now as the church are called to proclaim God's message to the world. All of us are called to be priests of God. We worship God, we pray to God, and we serve God. As a priest, we bring people to a saving knowledge of God as we represent God here as His ambassadors.

Peter says we are special people in four different ways.

Peter also says we are a "holy nation" another phrase from the Old Testament.[56] We are a chosen race of royal priests distinguished by our holiness. Earlier in his letter, Peter explains what God desires in terms of holiness. *"As obedient children, do not be conformed to the former lusts which were yours in your ignorance, but like the Holy One who called you, be holy yourselves also in all your behavior; because it is written, 'You shall be holy, for I am holy.'"*[57]

His admonition is similar to Paul's warning that we should not *"be conformed to this world"* but be transformed by the renewing of our minds.[58] An ambassador should not be conformed to the foreign culture. Neither should a Christian be conformed to our culture. Paul says we should *"see to it that no one takes you captive through philosophy and empty deception, according to the tradition of men, according to the elementary principles of the world, rather than according to Christ."*[59]

We should not try to blend in. We should not be taken captive by the culture. We should be set apart. That is what the term holy means. We should be different from the world.

Peter also says that we are "a people for his own possession." This descriptive title is also found in the Old Testament.[60] We are a chosen race of royal priests that are to be distinguished by holiness who are also identified as the people of God. Some translations say we are a "peculiar people." That doesn't mean we are to be peculiar in the sense of being weird.

But it does mean that we are "set apart" from the world. We are to be different from the world. The word for "possession" means "to purchase" or "to acquire for a price." It reminds us that we "*were bought with a price.*"[61] Christ paid that price on the cross. We are His prize and His possession.

Peter concludes by showing how our identity fits into God's purpose for us. Our purpose is to "proclaim the excellencies of Him who called us out of darkness into his marvelous light." The word "proclaim" here means to advertise or to promote. His "excellencies" illustrates the majestic and powerful work of God. The purpose of God's people as ambassadors is to witness to the greatness of God. We are chosen and empowered to proclaim Him through lives that testify to the goodness of God.

Peter also reminds us that God called us out of darkness and into the light. These are metaphors for sin and evil versus righteousness and goodness.[62] Once we were trapped in sin and rebellion. Now we are free and are called to proclaim this good news to those still trapped in darkness.

Peter emphasizes saying that we "*once were not a people, but now you are the people of God.*" This is a quote from the Old Testament book of Hosea.[63] Hosea's prophecy was directed toward the rebellious people in the Northern Kingdom of Israel, which would soon go into exile. But the prophecy also says there will come a time in which God will call them "my people."

Peter applies this not only to the Jewish people, but also to the Gentiles. All of us can be called "people of God" if we accept Jesus Christ as our Savior. In conversion, we become part of the family of God. God has not only given us a new identity. He has also given us a divine purpose based upon this identity. As we discussed in the previous chapter, we must go into the world and proclaim the excellencies of God.

We sow the seed. God brings the harvest.

Chapter 47: By Our Excellent Behavior

1 Pet. 2:11-12 *I urge you as aliens and strangers to abstain from fleshly lusts which wage war against the soul. Keep your behavior excellent among the Gentiles, so that in the thing in which they slander you as evildoers, they may because of your good deeds, as they observe them, glorify God in the day of visitation.*

Can we proclaim Christ's virtues through our behavior? Will people notice a difference? In the verse above, Peter says we can if we act as "aliens and strangers." These people have no legal status in the country where they are living. They are temporary residents. Their citizenship is elsewhere. Peter's expression matches Paul's teaching that "*our citizenship is in heaven.*"[64]

Peter admonishes them to "*abstain from fleshly lusts.*" Christians are holy people called to proclaim the goodness of God and His gospel.[65] One way to do this is through our excellent behavior. In other epistles, Paul provides several lists of fleshly desires[66] contrasting them with godly conduct.[67] He also contrasts the deeds of darkness with the deeds of light.[68] And he talks about our old nature and our new self.[69]

Note that not all fleshly desires are sexual. Many translations avoid using the word "lust" because it may imply that Peter is only talking about sexual sin. And we should also note that not all fleshly desires are sinful. We may desire food, but that is not sinful, but even that desire could lead to the excess of gluttony.

Peter reminds us that we live in a war zone. These lusts arise because we are still living in the flesh in a fallen world where sin prevails. As we discussed in a previous chapter on temptation, we should expect that this temptation would "war against the soul." That is why Paul says we are not to make "no provision for the flesh"[70] or "give the devil an opportunity."[71]

Peter therefore instructs us to live a life where our behavior is excellent. Other translations say we are to "conduct yourselves honorably." The Greek text uses a word that means winsome, attractive, or praiseworthy. He wants us to live a life pleasing to God, and pleasing to other people. Peter was challenging the Christians to live a life that was outwardly pleasing to their pagan neighbors. Likewise, we are to live our lives in a way that is a testimony to the watching world.

Sadly, that is not always the case. Perhaps you have heard people say, "I will never do business again with another Christian." Or you have heard people doubt the power of the gospel lamenting, "Christians live just like the world." We should be the most trustworthy, gracious, caring people on earth. We should live lives of integrity. Many of Paul's warnings to church leadership had to do with his concern about their behavior and how it looked to the secular world around them.[72]

Peter also warns that they will be unfairly attacked as critics *"slander them as evildoers."* Since the time of Peter, Christians have been slandered and persecuted for false reasons. They were accused of cannibalism, because they said during the Lord's Supper that *"this is my body."* They were accused of atheism because they did not worship idols. They were accused of treason because they would not say: "Caesar is Lord."

Your good deeds will be honored by all when Christ returns.

He concludes this section by pointing to *"the day of visitation"* when these critics will *"see your good works and glorify God."* Peter is speaking of the future when Jesus returns. Some who had been skeptical of the gospel will see our good works and become believers. Others will not believe but be forced to glorify God anyway.

Peter then gives instruction on how Christians are to act toward government and toward those around them in society:

> *Submit yourselves for the Lord's sake to every human institution, whether to a king . . ., or to governors as sent by*

> *him for the punishment of evildoers and the praise of those who do right. For such is the will of God that by doing right you may silence the ignorance of foolish men. . . . Honor all people, love the brotherhood, fear God, honor the king.*[73]

Peter admonishes them to submit to earthly authority. This may have been difficult for persecuted Christians to hear. They would have been more willing to resist or rebel rather than submit. Peter recognized that those in civil authority had the power to punish evildoers and "*praise those who do right.*" This is in agreement with Paul who taught: "*Every person is to be in subjection to the governing authorities. For there is no authority except from God, and those which exist are established by God.*"[74]

He goes on to argue that by their good behavior, they will be able to silence the slander of foolish men. Peter talks about "doing right" three times in this letter believing it will win others to Jesus Christ. From history, we know that was the case. Christianity went from being a few disciples to a world religion numbering over 30 million by the third century. Historians usually credit two things for that phenomenal growth. First, the good works that Christians did (serving others, helping the poor, treating people with dignity) was a visible testimony to the truth of the gospel. Second, the martyrdom of Christians caught their attention. A martyrs' death seemed supernatural to pagans and caused them to respect the Christian faith.[75]

Peter concludes by stating Christians are to "*honor everyone and love the brotherhood.*" We are to show honor and respect, starting first with those in authority over us but continuing on to every person. This concept was radical in that day when there were various classes of people including a mass in slavery. Peter, however, expected Christians to respect others and treat slaves and those in a lower class with respect and equality.

As strangers and aliens, exhibit excellent behavior.

Chapter 48: By our Right Relationships

1st Peter 2:21 *You have been called for this purpose, since Christ also suffered for you, leaving an example to follow in His steps.*

How are we to act as Christians toward other people? How will they be different from the world? Peter teaches we proclaim Christ through our right relationships.

> *Servants, be submissive to your masters with all respect, not only to those who are good and gentle, but also to those who are unreasonable. For this finds favor, if for the sake of conscience toward God a person bears up under sorrows when suffering unjustly.*[76]

You might be tempted to think that it has no relevance to us today. Peter was writing to servants who had masters. We don't have slavery, so how is his instruction relevant to us today? Although Peter does talk about servants and masters, the general principles apply to us today. We have people in authority over us, and we are to be submissive to those people. In fact, the term that Peter uses here is not a word restricted only to slaves but can be applied to the broader context of people who are under the authority of others.

We might also mention that the Bible does refer to believers as slaves and servants. Jesus taught: "*If anyone wants to be first, he shall be last of all and servant of all.*"[77] He drives the point home by then saying: "*whoever wishes to be first among you shall be slave of all.*"[78] Jesus refers to us as slaves and servants. Some commentators have said that another way to look at this passage is to consider it as the "worse case scenario." In other words, if the principle of submission applies to slavery in the Roman Empire, it surely applies to less difficult and demanding situations we find ourselves in today.

Earlier, Peter admonished us to submit to earthly authority. Here he tells us to be submissive to others who are in authority over us. That is certainly true for someone in the military, but it is also true for those of us in civilian life. We also have people in authority over us.

Peter says we are to be good and gentle, even if we have not been treated well by our boss or other people in authority. The way we live and how we respond to others is a powerful testimony and witness to the watching world. Peter also teaches us that we should be patient and persevere even when we are treated harshly and suffer unjustly.

Peter then points us back to Jesus Christ as our model of someone who suffered unjustly and provided a model for us.

> *For you have been called for this purpose, since Christ also suffered for you, leaving you an example for you to follow in His steps, who committed no sin, nor was any deceit found in his mouth and while being reviled, He did not revile in return; while suffering, He uttered no threats, but kept entrusting Himself to Him who judges righteously; and He Himself bore our sins . . . on the cross, so that we might die to sin and live to righteousness; for by His wounds you were healed.*[79]

Our attitude in the workplace should proclaim Christ.

Peter describes the suffering of Jesus Christ from Isaiah 53, a passage describing the "suffering servant." He also explains that we suffer because we "*have been called for this purpose.*" Also, we suffer because Christ suffered and died for us. Notice how Jesus Christ suffered. He suffered even though he "*committed no sin.*" He was righteous and "*no deceit [was] found in his mouth.*" Also, his suffering was silent: "*He uttered no threats.*" Instead, he entrusted "*Himself to Him who judges righteously.*" He bore our sins freeing us from the penalty of sin.

Finally, Peter admonishes believers to live lives of submission in marriage. Just as we are to submit to civil authority and those in authority over us, we should also submit to each other in marriage. Peter tells wives to *"be submissive to your own husbands so that even if any of them are disobedient to the word, they may be won without a word by the behavior of their wives."*[80] Living a life of submission can be a witness and testimony to others, including an unbelieving husband.

He also instructs husbands to *"live with your wives in an understanding way, as with someone weaker, since she is a woman; and show her honor as a fellow heir of the grace of life, so that your prayers will not be hindered."*[81] Husbands must seek to understand their wives. They should show her honor and respect. Christ-like marriages are a testimony desperately needed in the cheap sex society we live in.

Earlier, we mentioned the statement: "Be careful how you live; you will be the only Bible some people ever read." It is a reminder that our life and our actions may be the only contact many people will have with biblical principles. Live your life before the world in a way that testifies to the truth of the Bible.

As a Christian, your past should no longer define you. You have been changed. That is the theme of the song "Now I'm Bound" in the CD that accompanies this teaching series.[17]

Now I'm changed my past does not define me
I'm not the same I'm not held there anymore
Now I'm bound to liberty and freedom by the One who laid it down

Were the whole realm of nature mine; still an offering far too small
Love so amazing, so divine demands my life, my soul, my all
Demands my life, my soul, my all

In His name we're given the authority to overcome
All powers of the enemy. It's the love that conquers hell's ability
With the blood that sets captives free. In His name we'll set captives free.

Our marriages should proclaim Christ.

Chapter 49: By Our Defense of the Gospel

1st Peter 3:15 *always being ready to make a defense to everyone who asks you to give an account for the hope that is in you*

Throughout these chapters we have talked about the need for us to be freed from cultural captivity. We have learned that many have been taken *"captive through philosophy and empty deception, according to the tradition of men, according to the elementary principles of the world."*[82]

Not only should we be freed from cultural captivity, but we should also live victoriously in this new freedom in Christ. We are to *"walk in Him, having been firmly rooted and now being built up in Him and established in your faith."*[83] Our ultimate goal is to no longer live in captivity, but to be a confident ambassador for Jesus Christ. Paul reminds us that we are *"ambassadors for Christ."*[84]

One important aspect of being a confident ambassador is our ability to *"correctly handle the Word of truth.*[85] In order to be effective, we should be ready and able to defend God's Word. This is what Peter called for us to do:

> *But even if you should suffer for the sake of righteousness, you are blessed. And do not fear their intimidation, and do not be troubled, but sanctify Christ as Lord in your hearts, always being ready to make a defense to everyone who asks you to give an account for the hope that is in you, yet with gentleness and reverence; and keep a good conscience so that in the thing in which you are slandered, those who revile your good behavior in Christ will be put to shame.*[86]

Peter begins by emphasizing a theme we have discussed in earlier chapters. Christians were being persecuted. He reminds them that they should do what is good. It is always tempting to repay evil with evil.[87] But we as Christians are called to repay evil with good. Paul says: *"See that no one repays another with evil for evil, but always seek after that which is good for one another and for all people."*[88] In another letter Paul says: *"Let us not lose heart in doing good, for in due time we will reap if we do not grow weary. So then, while we have opportunity, let us do good to all people, and especially to those who are of the household of the faith."*[89]

Peter also acknowledges that suffering may continue: "even if you should suffer." Paul teaches us that we should not be surprised if suffering comes: *"For to you it has been granted for Christ's sake, not only to believe in Him, but also to suffer for His sake."*[90] Likewise, James explains that suffering will come and it will provide a test for our faith: *"Consider it all joy, my brethren, when you encounter various trials, knowing that the testing of your faith produces endurance. And let endurance have its perfect result, so that you may be perfect and complete, lacking in nothing."*[91]

After his initial teaching about how believers should be prepared for suffering, Peter then explains that we should also be prepared to defend the gospel. He begins by saying that we should "sanctify Christ." Other translations say we should "honor Christ." We honor or sanctify Christ by giving Him his place of honor in our lives. We do that by our worship of God and obedience to His commands. We honor him as holy and thus treat Him and our lives as separate from the world.

Be prepared to defend the truth of the gospel.

Always be ready to defend our faith; be constantly prepared. This comes from reading God's Word and our study of others who have been equipped to defend biblical truth. Have a teachable heart and be willing to learn from others who can help us become confident ambassadors for Christ.

Peter says we should be *"ready to make a defense."* The Greek word for defense is *apologia*. This is the root word for the term apologetics, the systematic defense of the Bible. In the Greek world, an *apologia* was a defense made in a court. Once defendants were accused, they would be allowed to refute the charges. The word means to "speak away" (*apo* means away, *logia* means speech). The defendants would dismiss by "speaking away" any charges against them. Peter is saying that when people attack the Bible or biblical doctrine, we are to "speak away" or refute what critics are saying.

Peter also explains that we have a responsibility "to give an account for the hope" that is in us. It assumes that we have hope even though we live in a world that lacks this hope. Earlier, Peter says we are "*born again to a living hope through the resurrection of Jesus Christ from the dead.*" This is the hope we are to be ready to defend.

Finally, Peter explains how to answer critics and skeptics. We are to respond with "gentleness and reverence." Our attitude is crucial. Sometimes we will be called upon to answer objections and criticisms. Other times we may merely be answering honest questions from seekers. In either case, we are to be meek, gentle, and respectful. It may be tempting to respond to angry critics with mean and cutting remarks. We are to respond to all the same kind way.

When we respond with grace and respect, Peter explains that: "*those who revile your good behavior in Christ will be put to shame.*" We have two weapons: truth and love. We should graciously respond to criticism by "*speaking the truth in love.*"[92] Throughout this book we have talked about the need to free ourselves from cultural captivity.[93] Once we do this, we are to develop into confident ambassadors[94] for Jesus Christ, able to handle God's Word[95] and to defend it.[96]

> *Defend with gentleness and respect*
> *cutting through their false expectations of Christians.*

OUR ETERNAL PURPOSE — Week One

[1] 2 Corinthians 4:16
[2] 1 Corinthians 15:31.
[3] 2 Corinthians 4:8.
[4] 2 Corinthians 4:1.
[5] 2 Corinthians 4:16.
[6] C.S. Lewis, *Mere Christianity* (New York: Harcourt Brace Jovanovich, 1974), 150.
[7] Ibid. 151.
[8] 2 Corinthians 4:17.
[9] Matthew 6:20.
[10] Romans 8:18.
[11] 1 Peter 1:7.
[12] C.S. Lewis, "The Weight of Glory," sermon delivered in Oxford in 1942, http://www.verber.com/mark/xian/weight-of-glory.pdf.
[13] 2 Corinthians 4:18.
[14] Hebrews 11:1.
[15] Matthew 6:20.
[16] "*Now I'm Bound*" Jennie Lee Riddle Music, 2010.
[17] Romans 8:22.
[18] Acts 18.
[19] 2 Corinthians 5:5.
[20] Hebrews 11:25.
[21] 1 Peter 2:9.
[22] Romans 8:28.
[23] 2 Corinthians 5:6.
[24] Philippians 1:21.
[25] 1 Peter 1:13.
[26] Colossians 3:2
[27] Philippians 3:13-14.
[28] 2 Corinthians 5:7-10.

DECEIVED BY THE FATHER OF LIES — Week Two

[1] John 8:44-45.
[2] John 12:31; 14:30; 16:11.
[3] Colossians 2:8.
[4] 2 Corinthians 4:4.
[5] Ephesians 2:2
[6] 1 John 5:19.
[7] 1 Peter 5:8.
[8] Colossians 2:6-7.
[9] Romans 3:23.
[10] Ephesians 2:8-9.

[11] Ephesians 6:12.
[12] 1 John 2:16.
[13] 1 Corinthians 3:10-11; Ephesians 2:20.
[14] Philippians 1:6.
[15] 1 John 3:1-3.
[16] John 14:6; Acts 4:12, Colossians 2:3; 2 Corinthians 12:9.
[17] C.S. Lewis, *Mere Christianity*, 43.
[18] Philippians 4:8.
[19] 1 Peter 5:8.
[20] Proverbs 29:3.
[21] Ephesians 5:6.
[22] 1 Corinthians 11:2.
[23] Matthew 15:3.
[24] Colossians 2:20.
[25] Galatians 4:3.
[26] John 14:6.
[27] Galatians 4:3
[28] Colossians 2:8.
[29] Galatians 4:3
[30] Colossians 2:16-17.
[31] Colossians 2:18-19.
[32] Colossians 2:20-23.
[33] 2 Corinthians 10:3-5.
[34] Matthew 7:15.
[35] Matthew 24:5.
[36] Galatians 1:8.
[37] 2 Peter 2:1.
[38] Acts 17:11.
[39] 2 Peter 2:2.
[40] 2 Peter 2:2.
[41] 2 Peter 2:3.
[42] Ephesians 6:10-13.
[43] 2 Corinthians 10:3-5.
[44] Ephesians 6:17.
[45] Colossian 1:13.
[46] Ephesians 6:11.
[47] Ephesians 6:12.
[48] Ephesians 6:14-17.
[49] 2 Timothy 2:15.
[50] Matthew 4, Mark 1, Luke 4
[51] 2 Peter 1:3
[52] Romans 6:12; 13:14.
[53] Romans 7:10-14.

EXPOSING FALSE VIEWS **Week Three**

[1] Harry Blamires, *The Christian Mind: How Should a Christian Think* (Ann Arbor, MI: Servant, 1963).
[2] Matthew 22:37.
[3] Nancy Pearcey, *Total Truth: Liberating Christianity from Its Cultural Captivity* (Wheaton, Ill.: Crossway Books, 2004).
[4] Christian Smith and Patricia Snell, *Souls in Transition: The Religious and Spiritual Lives of Emerging Adults* (New York: Oxford University Press, 2009).
[5] From General Social Surveys taken from 1976 through 2012
[6] *Culturally Captive Christian Study 2010*, research commissioned by Probe Ministries and conducted by Barna Group, 2010.
[7] Daniel Dennett, *Darwin's Dangerous Idea* (NY: Simon and Schuster, 1995), 63.
[8] George Gaylord Simpson, *The Meaning of Evolution* (New Haven: Yale University Press, 1967), 345.
[9] Psalm 139:13-16.
[10] Psalm 139:16.
[11] Acts 17:26.
[12] Colossians 1:15-17.
[13] Matthew 15:3.
[14] Matthew 23:28.
[15] Matthew 15:7; 16:3; 22:18; 23:23-29.
[16] 2 Timothy 3:5.
[17] Isaiah 64:6.
[18] Matthew 15:3-5.
[19] *National Study of Youth and Religion*, commissioned under the direction of Christian Smith, Department of Sociology, University of Notre Dame, www.youthandreligion.org.
[20] Romans 6:14.
[21] Acts 17:24.
[22] Galatians 5:1.
[23] Colossians 2:18-19.
[24] 1 Corinthians 12:1-3.
[25] Rhonda Byrne, *The Secret* (New York: Atria Books, 2006).
[26] Eckhart Tolle, *A New Earth: Awakening to Your Life's Purpose*, Penguin Group (New York, 2006).
[27] *National Study of Youth and Religion*
[28] Hebrews 5:14.
[29] Colossians 2:18.
[30] Colossians 2:20-23.
[31] Luke 9:23-24.
[32] Isaiah 64:6.
[33] Ephesians 2:8-9.
[34] Exodus 20:3-6; Deuteronomy 6:13-14.

[35] Galatians 1:8.
[36] 1 Timothy 2:5.
[37] Colossians 2:10.
[38] Colossians 2:8.
[39] Colossians 2:6.
[40] John 18:38.
[41] Richard Middleton and Brian Walsh, *Truth Is Stranger Than It Used to Be: Biblical Faith in a Postmodern Age* (Downers Grove, IL.: InterVarsity Press, 1995), 31.
[42] Genesis 3:1-24.
[43] John 14:6.
[44] Matthew 7:28-29.
[45] John 8:45-46.
[46] Ephesians 4:21.
[47] Phil Roberts, "On Mission," July/August 1999, 49.
[48] Steve Turner, *Nice and Nasty* (Marshall and Scott, 1980).
[49] John 14:6.
[50] *National Study of Youth and Religion*
[51] 2 Peter 3:19.
[52] Romans 3:23.
[53] Ephesians 2:8-9.

EXPOSING FALSE LIVING — Week Four

[1] Colossians 3:5-8.
[2] 1 Corinthians 6:9-11.
[3] *Culturally Captive Christian Study 2010, 40-41*
[4] Ibid., 42-49.
[5] Ibid., 50-51.
[6] Romans 12:2.
[7] 1 Peter 2:12.
[8] *Culturally Captive Christian Study 2010*, 57-63.
[9] James 1:20.
[10] Ephesians 4:26-27.
[11] Ephesians 4:15-19.
[12] 1 Corinthians 6:18.
[13] 1 Thessalonians 4:3-5.
[14] 1 Corinthians 10:13.
[15] Stephen Cable, *Cultural Captives: The Beliefs and Behavior of American Youth Adults* (Plano, TX: Probe Ministries, 2012), 167
[16] Proverbs 6:17.
[17] Romans 1:27-8, 1 Corinthians 6:9.
[18] 1 Thessalonians 4:3-5.
[19] 1 Corinthians 6:18-20.
[20] Galatians 5:19-21

[21] 1 John 1:9.
[22] 1 Peter 2:9-10.
[23] 1 Corinthians 6:18-20.
[24] 1 Corinthians 10:14.
[25] 2 Timothy 2:22.
[26] Proverbs 4:23.
[27] Job 31:1.
[28] Isaiah 33:15.
[29] Colossians 3:8.
[30] Philippians 4:8.
[31] Proverbs 1:10.
[32] Proverbs 1:15.
[33] 1 Peter 1:15-16.
[34] Romans 7:15, 19-20.
[35] A.W. Tozer, *Jesus, Author of Our Faith* (Christian Publications, 1911), 59.
[36] Colossians 3:5-7.
[37] Colossians 3:8.
[38] Colossians 3:9-11.
[39] C.S. Lewis, *Mere Christianity*, 166-167.
[40] Romans 6:5-6
[41] Galatians 2:20.
[42] Ephesians 4:22 (ESV).
[43] Ephesians 4:17.
[44] Ephesians 5:1-2.
[45] Ephesians 5:15-16.
[46] Ephesians 4:22-24.
[47] 2 Corinthians 4:16.
[48] Romans 8:29.
[49] Romans 12:2.
[50] 1 John 4:18-19
[51] Proverbs 9:10.
[52] Proverbs 3:7.
[53] Proverbs 19:23.
[54] Joshua 10:25.
[55] 1 Kings 17:13.
[56] Isaiah 41:13-14.
[57] Jeremiah 46:27.
[58] Daniel 10:12.
[59] Matthew 10:28-31; Luke 12:4-7.
[60] 2 Timothy 1:7 (KJV).
[61] Matthew 8:26.
[62] 1 John 2:5.
[63] 1 John 4:12.
[64] Romans 5:5.

[65] Philip Yancey, *What's So Amazing About Grace?* (Grand Rapids, MI: Zondervan, 1997), 45.
[66] Romans 10:9.

EMBRACING TRUE REALITY **Week Five**

[1] John 17:13-16.
[2] Ephesians 6:17.
[3] Psalm 119:9-10.
[4] Matthew 28:18-20.
[5] Ephesians 6:14-17.
[6] Colossians 2:8.
[7] Ephesians 6:12.
[8] Colossians 2:8.
[9] Philippians 4:8.
[10] 1 Corinthians 2:16.
[11] Proverbs 16:2.
[12] Mark 7:20-23.
[13] Jeremiah 17:9.
[14] James 1:13-15.
[15] Romans 8:29.
[16] Romans 12:2.
[17] Lamentations 3:23.
[18] Psalm 26:2; 139:23.
[19] Matthew 13; Mark 4; Luke 8.
[20] James 1:3-4.
[21] James 1:12.
[22] Romans 8:28.
[23] Psalm 66:10.
[24] 1 Peter 1:7.
[25] Proverbs 17:3.
[26] Psalm 26:2.
[27] 2 Chronicles 32:31.
[28] James 1:2-3.
[29] John 10:10
[30] John 16:33.
[31] 1 Peter 4:12.
[32] James 1:2-4.
[33] Acts 5:40-41; 16:23-25.
[34] Hebrews 12:2.
[35] 1 Peter 1:7.
[36] 1 Peter 5:7.
[37] 1 Corinthians 3:2-3.
[38] Romans 8:28.
[39] 1 Thessalonians 5:18.

[40] Mark 7:21-23.
[41] 1 Corinthians 10:12-13.
[42] Proverbs 4:23.
[43] Isaiah 29:13.
[44] 1 Corinthians 10:14.
[45] 1 Corinthians 6:8.
[46] Hebrews 4:15.
[47] Ephesians 4:27.
[48] Proverbs 4:26-27.
[49] James 1:12.
[50] Psalm 119;43, 151.
[51] John 17:17.
[52] 2 Timothy 3:16-17.
[53] Joshua 1:8.
[54] Psalm 77:12.
[55] Psalm 19:14
[56] Colossians 3:16.
[57] Psalm 119:105.
[58] Psalm 119:9.
[59] Deuteronomy 17:19.
[60] Psalm 119:97.
[61] Acts 1:8.
[62] 2 Timothy 2:2.
[63] Psalm 37:23
[64] Matthew 7:24.
[65] Romans 8:29.
[66] Philippians 1:6.
[67] Genesis 3:4.
[68] 2 Corinthians 4:4.
[69] Colossians 1:15.
[70] Colossians 2:9
[71] Romans 12:1-2.
[72] Matthew 4:20
[73] Mark 2:14.
[74] 1 Corinthians 11:1.
[75] Romans 6:11.
[76] 1 Peter 1:16.
[77] Romans 6:1-14.
[78] Psalm 119.
[79] Romans 8:34.
[80] Galatians 5:16.
[81] Colossians 1:28.
[82] 2 Peter 3:18.
[83] Ephesians 4:24.

[84] Ephesians 4:11-16.
[85] Ephesians 4:17-19.
[86] Ephesians 4:20-24.
[87] 2 Corinthians 3:18 (NIV).
[88] Philippians 2:13.
[89] Romans 12:2.
[90] Ephesians 4:23.
[91] John Stott, 'The Model – Becoming More like Christ.' Sermon delivered at the Keswick Convention 17 July 2007, http://www.langhampartnership.org/2007/08/06/john-stott-address-at-keswick.

Renewing in the Truth — Week Six

[1] Matthew 17:1-2.
[2] 2 Corinthians 5:17.
[3] Romans 8:29.
[4] 2 Corinthians 3:18.
[5] Joshua 1:8.
[6] Colossians 3:2
[7] Romans 15:13.
[8] Romans 12:1-2.
[9] 1 Kings 3:9.
[10] Proverbs 2:1-5.
[11] Philippians 1:9-10.
[12] 1 John 4:1.
[13] Hebrews 5:14.
[14] 1 John 2:15-17.
[15] Galatians 5:16.
[16] Luke 12:15.
[17] Proverbs 11:2.
[18] Proverbs 13:10.
[19] Proverbs 16:18.
[20] Ephesians 5:15-16.
[21] 2 Timothy 3:16.
[22] 2 Timothy 4:2.
[23] Galatians 6:1.
[24] James 1:17-18.
[25] Proverbs 30:5 (NIV).
[26] Psalm 33:4 (NIV).
[27] 1 Thessalonians 2:13.
[28] Genesis 1:28-30.
[29] Exodus 24, 32.
[30] Isaiah 8:1; 30:8; Jeremiah 25:13.
[31] Matthew 5:17-19; John 5:45; 10:33.

[32] 2 Timothy 3:16.
[33] John 7:16; 8:28; 12:49-50; 14:10, 24.
[34] John 14:26.
[35] J. Barton Payne, *Encyclopedia of Biblical Prophecy* (NY: Harper and Row), 681.
[36] Josh McDowell, *Evidence That Demands a Verdict* (San Bernardino, CA: Here's Life Publishers, 1979), 175.
[37] The Messiah will come through the line of Shem (Genesis 11), Abraham (Genesis 22), Isaac (Genesis 17), Jacob (Genesis 28), Judah (Genesis 49), Benjamin (Isaiah 11), and David (Isaiah 9:7).
[38] Micah 5:2.
[39] Zechariah 9:9.
[40] Zechariah 11:12-13.
[41] Psalm 22.
[42] Isaiah 53:9-12.
[43] Peter Stoner, *Science Speaks: Scientific Proof of the Accuracy of Prophecy and the Bible* (Chicago: Moody Press, 1963), 109-110.
[44] Acts 1:3.
[45] F. F. Bruce, *The New Testament Documents: Are They Reliable?* (Downers Grove, InterVarsity Press, 1983).
[46] Darrell Bock, *Who Is Jesus? Linking the Historical Jesus with the Christ of Faith* (NY: Howard Books, 2012).
[47] William Ramsay, *St. Paul the Traveler and the Roman Citizen* (Grand Rapids, MI: Baker Books, 1982), 8.
[48] Norman Geisler, *Baker Encyclopedia of Apologetics* (Grand Rapids, MI.: Baker Books, 1999), 47.
[49] 1 Peter 3:15.
[50] Acts 20:32.
[51] 2 Peter 1:3-4.
[52] 1 Peter 1:16.
[53] Matthew 5:48.
[54] John 15:3.
[55] John 17:17.
[56] Psalm 119:9.
[57] James 1:17-18.
[58] Proverbs 3:5 (NIV).
[59] 2 Timothy 3:16.
[60] John 15:4.
[61] 1 Peter 2:2.
[62] Matthew 4:4.
[63] 1 Corinthians 2:2.
[64] James 1:23.
[65] Matthew 7:24.
[66] 1 Corinthians 3:11.

[67] 2 Timothy 2:19 (NIV).
[68] Matthew 7:7-11.
[69] Ephesians 3:20.
[70] Matthew 21:22.
[71] Jamaes 4:2.
[72] James 1:17.
[73] Matthew 14:23.
[74] Luke 5:16.
[75] Matthew 26:36.
[76] Ephesians 6:19.
[77] Colossians 4:3-4.
[78] Philippians 1:9.
[79] Ephesians 3:16-17.
[80] Acts 2:42.
[81] Acts 6:4.
[82] Acts 6:5-6.
[83] Acts 13:3.
[84] Jude 1:20
[85] Luke 22:32.
[86] Luke 18:13.
[87] Matthew 9:38.
[88] Colossians 1:9-10.
[89] James 1:5-8.
[90] Philippians 4:6.
[91] James 5:16-20.
[92] 1 Thessalonians 5:17.

Our True Purpose in Life — Week Seven

[1] 1 Corinthians 12:12.
[2] Hebrews 10:25.
[3] Matthew 10:32.
[4] Psalm 100:2.
[5] John 4:24.
[6] Hebrews 10:25.
[7] Ephesians 5:19.
[8] Hebrews 10:24-25.
[9] Hebrews 13:17.
[10] 1 Peter 5:1-4.
[11] 1 Thessalonians 5:12-13
[12] 1 Corinthians 12.
[13] John 13:34-35.
[14] Romans 15:7.
[15] 1 Peter 4:9.
[16] James 5:16.

[17] 1 Thessalonians 4:18.
[18] 1 Thessalonians 5:11.
[19] Matthew 22:37-39.
[20] Matthew 6:15.
[21] 1 John 2:10.
[22] Matthew 12:49-50.
[23] Hebrews 2:11, NIV.
[24] 1 Corinthians 12:27.
[25] Ephesians 5:27.
[26] 1 John 2:9-10.
[27] John 13:35.
[28] Romans 12:4-5
[29] 1 Corinthians 12:12.
[30] 1 Corinthians 12:3-5.
[31] Ephesians 2:21-22.
[32] Ephesians 3:6.
[33] C.S. Lewis, Paper read on "Membership," 10 February 1945, copyright © 1975, 1980 by The Trustees of the Estate of C.S. Lewis.
[34] John 13:34-35; 15:12, 17; 1 John 3:23; 4:7, 11-12.
[35] James 5:16.
[36] 1 Thessalonians 4:18; 5:11
[37] Hebrews 3:13; 10:25.
[38] Ephesians 4:32; Colossians 3:13.
[39] Colossians 3:16.
[40] Philippians 4:19.
[41] 1 John 3:2.
[42] 2 Corinthians 3:18
[43] Revelation 21:4.
[44] Romans 8:17.
[45] 1 Peter 1:3-4.
[46] Matthew 5:14-16.
[47] Matthew 28:18-20.
[48] 2 Corinthians 5:20.
[49] 1 Peter 3:15.
[50] Acts 1:8.
[51] John 6:44.
[52] 2 Corinthians 5:20.
[53] Deuteronomy 7:6; 10:15; Isaiah 43:20-21.
[54] 1 Peter 2:5.
[55] Exodus 19:6; Isaiah 61:6; 66:21.
[56] Exodus 19:6; Deuteronomy 7:6.
[57] 1 Peter 1:14-16
[58] Romans 12:1.
[59] Colossians 2:8.

[60] Exodus 19:5; Deuteronomy 4:20; 7:6; 14:2; 26:18; Malachi 3:17.
[61] 1 Corinthians 6:20.
[62] John 3:19-21; Acts 16:18.
[63] Hosea 1:10; 2:23.
[64] Philippians 3:20.
[65] 1 Peter 2:9-10.
[66] Galatians 5:19-21.
[67] Galatians 5:22-23.
[68] Ephesians 5:8-14.
[69] Colossians 3:5-10.
[70] Romans 13:14.
[71] Ephesians 4:27.
[72] 1 Thessalonians 4:11-12; 1 Corinthians 10:32.
[73] 1 Peter 2:13-17.
[74] Romans 12:1.
[75] Rodney Stark, *The Triumph of Christianity: How the Jesus Movement Became the World's Largest Religion* (NY: Harper, 2011), 151.
[76] 1 Peter 2:18-20.
[77] Mark 9:35.
[78] Mark 10:44.
[79] 1 Peter 2:21-25.
[80] 1 Peter 3:1-2.
[81] 1 Peter 3:7.
[82] Colossians 2:8.
[83] Colossians 2:6-7.
[84] 2 Corinthians 5:20.
[85] 2 Timothy 2:15.
[86] 1 Peter 3:13-16.
[87] 1 Peter 3:9.
[88] 1 Thessalonians 5:15.
[89] Galatians 6:9-10.
[90] Philippians 1:29.
[91] James 1:2-4.
[92] Ephesians 4:15.
[93] Colossians 2:8.
[94] 2 Corinthians 5:20.
[95] 2 Timothy 2:15.
[96] 1 Peter 3:15-16.

Made in the USA
Lexington, KY
31 January 2018